The BIBLE Promise Book®

500 Scriptures to Bless a Woman's Heart

The BIBLE Promise Book®

500 Scriptures to Bless a Woman's Heart

Written and Compiled by
Jessie Fioritto

BARBOUR BOOKS
An Imprint of Barbour Publishing, Inc.

Published by Barbour Books, an imprint of Barbour Publishing Inc., 1810 Barbour Drive, Uhrichsville, Ohio 44683, www.barbourbooks.com

Our mission is to inspire the world with the life-changing message of the Bible.

 Member of the
Evangelical Christian
Publishers Association

Printed in the United States of America.

CONTENTS

ADOPTED

Father in heaven, You truly are my Father. You have delivered me from slavery to sin and signed my adoption papers with the blood of Jesus' sacrifice. I am Your beloved daughter. You've removed my filthy rags and gifted me with an eternal inheritance as a child of the high King of heaven. Sometimes the trials of this world threaten to crush me, and I'm tempted to lose hope. Keep my eyes focused on the glory that is to come so I can walk virtuously as Your daughter. In Jesus' precious name, amen.

1.

Giving thanks unto the Father, which hath made us meet to be partakers of the inheritance of the saints in light: Who hath delivered us from the power of darkness, and hath translated us into the kingdom of his dear Son.

COLOSSIANS 1:12–13

2.

Jesus answered, My kingdom is not of this world: if my kingdom were of this world, then would my servants fight, that I should not be delivered to the Jews: but now is my kingdom not from hence.

JOHN 18:36

3.

But as many as received him, to them
gave he power to become the sons of God,
even to them that believe on his name: Which
were born, not of blood, nor of the will of the
flesh, nor of the will of man, but of God.

JOHN 1:12–13

———•———————•———

4.

For as many as are led by the Spirit of God,
they are the sons of God. For ye have not
received the spirit of bondage again to fear;
but ye have received the Spirit of adoption,
whereby we cry, Abba, Father.

ROMANS 8:14–15

———•———————•———

5.

We are the children of God: And if children, then
heirs; heirs of God, and joint-heirs with Christ;
if so be that we suffer with him, that we may be also
glorified together. For I reckon that the sufferings
of this present time are not worthy to be compared
with the glory which shall be revealed in us.

ROMANS 8:16–18

6.

For we know that the whole creation groaneth
and travaileth in pain together until now. And
not only they, but ourselves also, which have the
firstfruits of the Spirit, even we ourselves groan
within ourselves, waiting for the adoption,
to wit, the redemption of our body.

ROMANS 8:22–23

7.

That ye may be blameless and harmless, the sons
of God, without rebuke, in the midst of a crooked
and perverse nation, among whom ye shine as
lights in the world; Holding forth the word of life.

PHILIPPIANS 2:15–16

8.

Beloved, now are we the sons of God, and it
doth not yet appear what we shall be: but we
know that, when he shall appear, we shall be
like him; for we shall see him as he is.

1 JOHN 3:2

9.

For ye are all the children of God by faith in Christ Jesus. For as many of you as have been baptized into Christ have put on Christ.

GALATIANS 3:26–27

10.

He hath chosen us in him before the foundation of the world, that we should be holy and without blame before him in love: Having predestinated us unto the adoption of children by Jesus Christ to himself, according to the good pleasure of his will, To the praise of the glory of his grace, wherein he hath made us accepted in the beloved.

EPHESIANS 1:4–6

ANXIETY

God, sometimes my fears well up inside of me. Life seems uncertain and scary and dark. But You know my needs and offer me protection. You have promised never to leave my side. Help me to remember that prayer and thanksgiving are the antidotes to my anxious thoughts. Fill my mind with Your peace that is beyond understanding. Take away my fear and replace it with an attitude of power and love, because You have called me by name and I belong to You. In the name of Jesus, amen.

11.

Be careful for nothing; but in every thing
by prayer and supplication with thanksgiving
let your requests be made known unto God.
And the peace of God, which passeth all
understanding, shall keep your hearts and
minds through Christ Jesus.

PHILIPPIANS 4:6–7

12.

Humble yourselves therefore under
the mighty hand of God, that he may
exalt you in due time: Casting all your
care upon him; for he careth for you.

1 PETER 5:6–7

13.

Wherefore, if God so clothe the grass of the field, which to day is, and to morrow is cast into the oven, shall he not much more clothe you, O ye of little faith? Therefore take no thought, saying, What shall we eat? or, What shall we drink? or, Wherewithal shall we be clothed?

MATTHEW 6:30–31

14.

Take therefore no thought for the morrow: for the morrow shall take thought for the things of itself. Sufficient unto the day is the evil thereof.

MATTHEW 6:34

15.

I know both how to be abased, and I know how to abound: every where and in all things I am instructed both to be full and to be hungry, both to abound and to suffer need. I can do all things through Christ which strengtheneth me.

PHILIPPIANS 4:12–13

16.

The God of all grace, who hath called us unto
his eternal glory by Christ Jesus, after that ye
have suffered a while, make you perfect,
stablish, strengthen, settle you.

1 PETER 5:10

17.

Have not I commanded thee? Be strong and
of a good courage; be not afraid, neither be
thou dismayed: for the LORD thy God is with
thee whithersoever thou goest.

JOSHUA 1:9

18.

Peace I leave with you, my peace I give unto you:
not as the world giveth, give I unto you. Let not
your heart be troubled, neither let it be afraid.

JOHN 14:27

19.

For God hath not given us the spirit of fear;
but of power, and of love, and of a sound mind.

2 Timothy 1:7

——•————————————•——

20.

Fear not: for I have redeemed thee, I have
called thee by thy name; thou art mine.
When thou passest through the waters,
I will be with thee; and through the rivers,
they shall not overflow thee.

Isaiah 43:1–2

BELIEF

Lord Jesus, the world says that You were just a man—
a charismatic teacher who rattled the status quo and
forged history. But my heart cries out that there's so much
more to Your story. I believe, Jesus, that You are God's
beloved Son, the God-man who walked blamelessly and
died in my place only to rise again. My heart shouts as
Mary did to the disciples three days after the horror of
Your death: Jesus is alive! Lord, crush every doubt and let
me live each moment in the breathtaking power of belief.
Amen.

21.

Let not your heart be troubled:
ye believe in God, believe also in me.

JOHN 14:1

———•————————————•———

22.

That if thou shalt confess with thy mouth the
Lord Jesus, and shalt believe in thine heart
that God hath raised him from the dead, thou
shalt be saved. For with the heart man believeth
unto righteousness; and with the mouth
confession is made unto salvation.

ROMANS 10:9–10

23.

Jesus saith unto her, Said I not
unto thee, that, if thou wouldest believe,
thou shouldest see the glory of God?

JOHN 11:40

24.

For what saith the scripture? Abraham
believed God, and it was counted unto
him for righteousness. Now to him that
worketh is the reward not reckoned of grace,
but of debt. But to him that worketh not,
but believeth on him that justifieth the ungodly,
his faith is counted for righteousness.

ROMANS 4:3–5

25.

Sirs, what must I do to be saved? And
they said, Believe on the Lord Jesus Christ,
and thou shalt be saved, and thy house.

ACTS 16:30–31

26.

In whom ye also trusted, after that ye heard
the word of truth, the gospel of your salvation:
in whom also after that ye believed, ye were
sealed with that holy Spirit of promise,
Which is the earnest of our inheritance until
the redemption of the purchased possession,
unto the praise of his glory.

EPHESIANS 1:13–14

27.

Jesus said unto him, If thou canst believe,
all things are possible to him that believeth.

MARK 9:23

28.

Now the God of hope fill you with all joy and
peace in believing, that ye may abound in hope,
through the power of the Holy Ghost.

ROMANS 15:13

29.

For whatsoever is born of God overcometh
the world: and this is the victory that
overcometh the world, even our faith.
Who is he that overcometh the world, but he
that believeth that Jesus is the Son of God?

1 JOHN 5:4–5

30.

And straightway the father of the child
cried out, and said with tears, Lord,
I believe; help thou mine unbelief.

MARK 9:24

BITTERNESS

God, excise the bitterness from my heart and implant Your love that covers all wrongs. I have been wounded by others, but I long to release my pain and anger to You and submit to Your physician's hand on my bruised heart. I know that trudging into the swamp of bitterness leads to my own destruction, but the path of forgiveness brings life. I choose life. I choose freedom. I will no longer glory in my offenses and foster bitterness toward others; instead I will glory in overlooking slights and forgiving as You have forgiven me. In Jesus' name, amen.

31.

Let all bitterness, and wrath, and anger, and clamour, and evil speaking, be put away from you, with all malice: And be ye kind one to another, tenderhearted, forgiving one another, even as God for Christ's sake hath forgiven you.

EPHESIANS 4:31–32

32.

Follow peace with all men, and holiness, without which no man shall see the Lord: Looking diligently lest any man fail of the grace of God; lest any root of bitterness springing up trouble you, and thereby many be defiled.

HEBREWS 12:14–15

33.

For if ye forgive men their trespasses,
your heavenly Father will also forgive you:
But if ye forgive not men their trespasses,
neither will your Father forgive your trespasses.

MATTHEW 6:14–15

34.

Hatred stirreth up strifes:
but love covereth all sins.

PROVERBS 10:12

35.

If it be possible, as much as lieth in you,
live peaceably with all men. Dearly beloved,
avenge not yourselves, but rather give place
unto wrath: for it is written, Vengeance is
mine; I will repay, saith the Lord.

ROMANS 12:18–19

36.

Who is a wise man and endued with knowledge
among you? let him shew out of a good
conversation his works with meekness of wisdom.
But if ye have bitter envying and strife in your
hearts, glory not, and lie not against the truth.

JAMES 3:13–14

37.

The discretion of a man deferreth his anger;
and it is his glory to pass over a transgression.

PROVERBS 19:11

38.

To the Lord our God belong mercies
and forgivenesses, though we
have rebelled against him.

DANIEL 9:9

39.

So wilt thou recover me, and make me to
live. Behold, for peace I had great bitterness:
but thou hast in love to my soul delivered
it from the pit of corruption: for thou hast
cast all my sins behind thy back.

ISAIAH 38:16–17

40.

So when they continued asking him, he lifted up
himself, and said unto them, He that is without
sin among you, let him first cast a stone at her.

JOHN 8:7

BLESSINGS

Heavenly Father, why is my focus so often centered on my problems, my failures, and every little detail that doesn't go my way? Why do I miss the sea of blessings I'm drowning in? Blessings showered down by a gracious and loving God. Lord, I'm blessed! I have breath to praise You and eternal life with You ahead of me. What are a few minor discomforts along the way in comparison to the richness of walking in Your truth? Thank You, Jesus, for every good thing that comes to me, because You are the origin of all goodness. Amen.

41.

Happy is he that hath the God of Jacob for his help, whose hope is in the Lord his God: Which made heaven, and earth, the sea, and all that therein is: which keepeth truth for ever.

Psalm 146:5–6

42.

But my God shall supply all your need according to his riches in glory by Christ Jesus. Now unto God and our Father be glory for ever and ever. Amen.

Philippians 4:19–20

43.

If thou shalt hearken diligently unto the voice of the LORD thy God, to observe and to do all his commandments which I command thee this day, that the LORD thy God will set thee on high above all nations of the earth: And all these blessings shall come on thee, and overtake thee.

DEUTERONOMY 28:1–2

44.

And of his fulness have all we received, and grace for grace.

JOHN 1:16

45.

But as it is written, Eye hath not seen, nor ear heard, neither have entered into the heart of man, the things which God hath prepared for them that love him.

1 CORINTHIANS 2:9

46.

And we know that all things work together
for good to them that love God, to them who
are the called according to his purpose.

Romans 8:28

47.

Your heavenly Father knoweth that ye have need
of all these things. But seek ye first the kingdom
of God, and his righteousness; and all these
things shall be added unto you.

Matthew 6:32–33

48.

For I will pour water upon him that is thirsty,
and floods upon the dry ground: I will pour my
spirit upon thy seed, and my blessing upon thine
offspring: And they shall spring up as among the
grass, as willows by the water courses.

Isaiah 44:3–4

49.

Fear not, O land; be glad and rejoice:
for the LORD will do great things.

JOEL 2:21

50.

Bless the LORD, O my soul, and forget not all his
benefits: Who forgiveth all thine iniquities; who
healeth all thy diseases; Who redeemeth thy life
from destruction; who crowneth thee with
lovingkindness and tender mercies.

PSALM 103:2–4

51.

Every good gift and every perfect gift is from
above, and cometh down from the Father of
lights, with whom is no variableness, neither
shadow of turning. Of his own will begat he us
with the word of truth, that we should be
a kind of firstfruits of his creatures.

JAMES 1:17–18

COMFORT

God Almighty, terrifying storms have whipped the turbulent waters of my life into a roaring frenzy. Like Peter who stepped out of his boat to come after You, I'm tempted to shift my eyes from You as You walk above the tossing waves. But Your promises comfort me. You offer me hope and forgiveness and help in the midst of my problems. You offer comfort for my fear-wracked soul. You are the God of all comfort. Help me also to extend a soothing balm to the wounded world around me. In Jesus' name, amen.

52.

Blessed be God, even the Father of our Lord Jesus Christ, the Father of mercies, and the God of all comfort; Who comforteth us in all our tribulation, that we may be able to comfort them which are in any trouble, by the comfort wherewith we ourselves are comforted of God.

2 CORINTHIANS 1:3–4

53.

Yea, though I walk through the valley of the shadow of death, I will fear no evil: for thou art with me; thy rod and thy staff they comfort me.

PSALM 23:4

54.

Seeing the multitudes, he went up into a mountain: and when he was set, his disciples came unto him: And he opened his mouth, and taught them, saying, Blessed are the poor in spirit: for theirs is the kingdom of heaven. Blessed are they that mourn: for they shall be comforted.

MATTHEW 5:1–4

55.

Remember the word unto thy servant, upon which thou hast caused me to hope. This is my comfort in my affliction: for thy word hath quickened me. The proud have had me greatly in derision: yet have I not declined from thy law.

PSALM 119:49–51

56.

Comfort ye, comfort ye my people, saith your God. Speak ye comfortably to Jerusalem, and cry unto her, that her warfare is accomplished, that her iniquity is pardoned: for she hath received of the LORD's hand double for all her sins.

ISAIAH 40:1–2

57.

And ye now therefore have sorrow: but I will
see you again, and your heart shall rejoice,
and your joy no man taketh from you.

JOHN 16:22

58.

Sing, O heavens; and be joyful, O earth;
and break forth into singing, O mountains:
for the LORD hath comforted his people,
and will have mercy upon his afflicted.

ISAIAH 49:13

59.

As one whom his mother comforteth, so will
I comfort you; and ye shall be comforted in
Jerusalem. And when ye see this, your heart shall
rejoice, and your bones shall flourish like an herb.

ISAIAH 66:13–14

60.

He shall feed his flock like a shepherd:
he shall gather the lambs with his arm,
and carry them in his bosom, and shall
gently lead those that are with young.

ISAIAH 40:11

———•————————————————•—

61.

He that dwelleth in the secret place of the most
High shall abide under the shadow of the
Almighty. I will say of the LORD, He is my refuge
and my fortress: my God; in him will I trust.

PSALM 91:1–2

COMPASSION

Jesus, too often I deal in judgment instead of mercy. I see someone stumbling or messing up and I think, What is their problem? I see their failure, but I miss the pain and brokenness causing their missteps. Jesus, open my eyes! Help me to see others through the lens of Your love. Move me with compassion for those wandering sheep who haven't encountered their Shepherd. It may be easier and more comfortable to look away from others' painful and messy lives, but You have called Your children to love. Forgive me for my hardened heart, Father. Amen.

62.

And Jesus, when he came out, saw much people, and was moved with compassion toward them, because they were as sheep not having a shepherd: and he began to teach them many things.

Mark 6:34

63.

Can a woman forget her sucking child, that she should not have compassion on the son of her womb? yea, they may forget, yet will I not forget thee.

Isaiah 49:15

64.

But whoso hath this world's good, and seeth
his brother have need, and shutteth up
his bowels of compassion from him,
how dwelleth the love of God in him?

1 John 3:17

65.

But when he saw the multitudes, he was
moved with compassion on them, because
they fainted, and were scattered abroad,
as sheep having no shepherd.

Matthew 9:36

66.

Though I have the gift of prophecy, and
understand all mysteries, and all knowledge;
and though I have all faith, so that I could remove
mountains, and have not charity, I am nothing.

1 Corinthians 13:2

67.

Bless the LORD, O my soul, and forget not all
his benefits: Who forgiveth all thine iniquities;
who healeth all thy diseases; Who redeemeth thy
life from destruction; who crowneth thee with
lovingkindness and tender mercies.

PSALM 103:2–4

68.

Pure religion and undefiled before God
and the Father is this, To visit the fatherless
and widows in their affliction, and to keep
himself unspotted from the world.

JAMES 1:27

69.

Rejoice with them that do rejoice,
and weep with them that weep.

ROMANS 12:15

70.

Put on therefore, as the elect of God, holy
and beloved, bowels of mercies, kindness,
humbleness of mind, meekness, longsuffering.

COLOSSIANS 3:12

71.

But he, being full of compassion, forgave their
iniquity, and destroyed them not: yea, many a
time turned he his anger away, and did not stir
up all his wrath. For he remembered that they
were but flesh; a wind that passeth away,
and cometh not again.

PSALM 78:38–39

CONFIDENCE

Lord, at times I feel small—too small and broken to be worthy or used by You. Remove my timid spirit and fill me with the confidence of young David when he faced down the giant Goliath. His boldness originated with You. And my sufficiency comes from You, not myself. Jesus, You opened the way for the wretched and unworthy to approach God's throne of grace with confidence in our forgiveness. I am washed clean and, like David, backed by the armies of the Most High. Make me bold. In the name of Jesus, amen.

72.

Be not afraid of sudden fear, neither of the
desolation of the wicked, when it cometh.
For the LORD shall be thy confidence,
and shall keep thy foot from being taken.
PROVERBS 3:25–26

73.

Fear thou not; for I am with thee: be not
dismayed; for I am thy God: I will strengthen
thee; yea, I will help thee; yea, I will uphold
thee with the right hand of my righteousness.
ISAIAH 41:10

74.

Not that we are sufficient of ourselves
to think any thing as of ourselves;
but our sufficiency is of God.

2 Corinthians 3:5

75.

For he hath said, I will never leave thee,
nor forsake thee. So that we may boldly say,
The Lord is my helper, and I will not
fear what man shall do unto me.

Hebrews 13:5–6

76.

I can do all things through Christ
which strengtheneth me.

Philippians 4:13

77.

The LORD is my light and my salvation; whom
shall I fear? the LORD is the strength of my life;
of whom shall I be afraid? . . . Though war should
rise against me, in this will I be confident.

PSALM 27:1, 3

78.

In the fear of the LORD is strong confidence:
and his children shall have a place of refuge.

PROVERBS 14:26

79.

Knowing in yourselves that ye have in heaven
a better and an enduring substance. Cast not
away therefore your confidence, which
hath great recompence of reward.

HEBREWS 10:34–35

80.

Having therefore, brethren, boldness to enter
into the holiest by the blood of Jesus, By a new
and living way, which he hath consecrated for us,
through the veil, that is to say, his flesh.

HEBREWS 10:19–20

81.

Let us therefore come boldly unto the
throne of grace, that we may obtain mercy,
and find grace to help in time of need.

HEBREWS 4:16

COURAGE

God, life can be scary. It's unpredictable at best, and the only sure thing seems to be that storms will come my way. But You, the living and almighty God, have promised to stay with me. Sweep away my fear and infuse me with power, love, and sound thinking. I trust in You, God, and not in the power of my own understanding. I know that if I follow You in obedience, You will guide and direct me. None can stand against me and no circumstance can shake me when I am backed by Your mighty hand. Amen.

82.

For God hath not given us the spirit of fear;
but of power, and of love, and of a sound mind.
Be not thou therefore ashamed of the testimony
of our Lord, nor of me his prisoner: but be
thou partaker of the afflictions of the gospel
according to the power of God.

2 TIMOTHY 1:7–8

83.

Trust in the LORD with all thine heart; and lean not
unto thine own understanding. In all thy ways
acknowledge him, and he shall direct thy paths.

PROVERBS 3:5–6

84.

Thou art my servant; I have chosen thee, and not cast thee away. Fear thou not; for I am with thee: be not dismayed; for I am thy God: I will strengthen thee; yea, I will help thee; yea, I will uphold thee with the right hand of my righteousness.

Isaiah 41:9–10

85.

O Lord, I will praise thee: though thou wast angry with me, thine anger is turned away, and thou comfortedst me. Behold, God is my salvation; I will trust, and not be afraid: for the Lord Jehovah is my strength and my song; he also is become my salvation.

Isaiah 12:1–2

86.

If God be for us, who can be against us? He that spared not his own Son, but delivered him up for us all, how shall he not with him also freely give us all things? Who shall lay any thing to the charge of God's elect? It is God that justifieth.

Romans 8:31–33

87.

Be of good courage, and he shall strengthen
your heart, all ye that hope in the LORD.

PSALM 31:24

88.

The wicked flee when no man pursueth:
but the righteous are bold as a lion.

PROVERBS 28:1

89.

In all these things we are more than conquerors
through him that loved us. For I am persuaded,
that neither death, nor life, nor angels, nor
principalities, nor powers, nor things present,
nor things to come, Nor height, nor depth,
nor any other creature, shall be able to
separate us from the love of God.

ROMANS 8:37–39

90.

Be strong in the Lord, and in the power
of his might. Put on the whole armour
of God, that ye may be able to stand
against the wiles of the devil.

EPHESIANS 6:10–11

91.

And all this assembly shall know that the LORD
saveth not with sword and spear: for the battle is
the LORD's, and he will give you into our hands.

1 SAMUEL 17:47

ENCOURAGEMENT

*Heavenly Father, help me to speak life into the lives
of others. I want to be known as an encourager rather
than a critic. Guard my lips from gossip and negative
comments, and instead instill my words with grace and
compassion. Show me the overlooked people around
me who are stoop-shouldered and weary beneath their
burdens. Jesus, You lifted all of my burdens and took
them upon Yourself, and now it's my desire to lighten
another's load. Give me the words to uplift and actions
to encourage others. In Jesus' name, amen.*

92.
Wherefore comfort yourselves together,
and edify one another, even as also ye do.
And we beseech you, brethren, to know
them which labour among you, and are
over you in the Lord, and admonish you.
1 Thessalonians 5:11–12

—————•———————•———

93.
Now we exhort you, brethren, warn them that are
unruly, comfort the feebleminded, support the weak,
be patient toward all men. See that none render evil
for evil unto any man; but ever follow that which is
good, both among yourselves, and to all men.
1 Thessalonians 5:14–15

94.

And let us consider one another to provoke
unto love and to good works: Not forsaking the
assembling of ourselves together, as the manner
of some is; but exhorting one another: and so
much the more, as ye see the day.

Hebrews 10:24–25

95.

For whatsoever things were written
aforetime were written for our learning,
that we through patience and comfort
of the scriptures might have hope.

Romans 15:4

96.

With one mind and one mouth glorify God,
even the Father of our Lord Jesus Christ.
Wherefore receive ye one another, as Christ
also received us to the glory of God.

Romans 15:6–7

97.

Let no corrupt communication proceed out of your mouth, but that which is good to the use of edifying, that it may minister grace unto the hearers. And grieve not the holy Spirit of God, whereby ye are sealed unto the day of redemption.

EPHESIANS 4:29–30

98.

But they that wait upon the LORD shall renew their strength; they shall mount up with wings as eagles; they shall run, and not be weary; and they shall walk, and not faint.

ISAIAH 40:31

99.

But exhort one another daily, while it is called To day; lest any of you be hardened through the deceitfulness of sin. For we are made partakers of Christ, if we hold the beginning of our confidence stedfast unto the end.

HEBREWS 3:13–14

100.

We then that are strong ought to bear the infirmities of the weak, and not to please ourselves. Let every one of us please his neighbour for his good to edification. For even Christ pleased not himself.

ROMANS 15:1–3

—•————————————•—

101.

Let us therefore follow after the things which make for peace, and things wherewith one may edify another.

ROMANS 14:19

ETERNAL GOD

*Lord God, it's incredible to think that You have always
been and You always will be. You never change. Your
love and grace and power and might are forever. Jesus,
I'm humbled and awed that You gave Yourself so that I
can live eternally with my heavenly Father. When I'm
consumed with worry, I need only to remember that You
are constant and own all the wisdom of the ages. My
help comes from You, the everlasting, all-powerful God.
I trust in You. In the name of Your Son, Jesus, amen.*

102.

Hast thou not known? hast thou not heard, that
the everlasting God, the LORD, the Creator of the
ends of the earth, fainteth not, neither is weary?
there is no searching of his understanding.

ISAIAH 40:28

103.

Lord, thou hast been our dwelling place in
all generations. Before the mountains were
brought forth, or ever thou hadst formed the
earth and the world, even from everlasting
to everlasting, thou art God.

PSALM 90:1–2

104.

Who is the blessed and only Potentate, the
King of kings, and Lord of lords; Who only
hath immortality, dwelling in the light which
no man can approach unto; whom no man
hath seen, nor can see: to whom be honour
and power everlasting. Amen.

1 TIMOTHY 6:15–16

105.

For the invisible things of him from the creation
of the world are clearly seen, being understood by
the things that are made, even his eternal power
and Godhead; so that they are without excuse.

ROMANS 1:20

106.

I am Alpha and Omega, the beginning
and the end, the first and the last.

REVELATION 22:13

107.

How much more shall the blood of Christ,
who through the eternal Spirit offered himself
without spot to God, purge your conscience
from dead works to serve the living God?

HEBREWS 9:14

108.

Now unto the King eternal, immortal,
invisible, the only wise God, be honour
and glory for ever and ever. Amen.

1 TIMOTHY 1:17

109.

For thus saith the high and lofty One that
inhabiteth eternity, whose name is Holy;
I dwell in the high and holy place, with him
also that is of a contrite and humble spirit,
to revive the spirit of the humble, and to
revive the heart of the contrite ones.

ISAIAH 57:15

110.

Who hath wrought and done it, calling the
generations from the beginning? I the LORD,
the first, and with the last; I am he.

ISAIAH 41:4

———•————————————•———

111.

There is none like unto the God of Jeshurun, who
rideth upon the heaven in thy help, and in his
excellency on the sky. The eternal God is thy
refuge, and underneath are the everlasting arms.

DEUTERONOMY 33:26–27

FAILURE

God, sometimes I don't win. Sometimes I don't succeed, and my frustrated efforts mock me. Failure threatens to pull me under the dark waters of despair. I don't understand why I wasn't enough, but I'm left feeling inadequate, defeated, unworthy. But it has been said that we don't truly understand grace until we fall— until we are caught by Your grace. Lord, You accomplish Your will even through my failure. All You ask is that I persevere. Although I may not always understand why things happen, I trust in Your goodness, love, and mercy. In Jesus' name, amen.

112.

Likewise the Spirit also helpeth our infirmities: for we know not what we should pray for as we ought: but the Spirit itself maketh intercession for us with groanings which cannot be uttered.

ROMANS 8:26

113.

And he that searcheth the hearts knoweth what is the mind of the Spirit, because he maketh intercession for the saints according to the will of God. And we know that all things work together for good to them that love God, to them who are the called according to his purpose.

ROMANS 8:27–28

114.

My grace is sufficient for thee: for my strength
is made perfect in weakness. Most gladly
therefore will I rather glory in my infirmities,
that the power of Christ may rest upon me.

2 Corinthians 12:9

115.

Trust in the Lord with all thine heart;
and lean not unto thine own understanding.
In all thy ways acknowledge him,
and he shall direct thy paths.

Proverbs 3:5–6

116.

My flesh and my heart faileth: but God is the
strength of my heart, and my portion for ever.

Psalm 73:26

117.

Therefore if any man be in Christ, he is
a new creature: old things are passed away;
behold, all things are become new.

2 Corinthians 5:17

118.

Being confident of this very thing, that he
which hath begun a good work in you will
perform it until the day of Jesus Christ.

Philippians 1:6

119.

Put off concerning the former conversation
the old man, which is corrupt according to
the deceitful lusts; And be renewed in the
spirit of your mind; And that ye put on the
new man, which after God is created in
righteousness and true holiness.

Ephesians 4:22–24

120.

This one thing I do, forgetting those things which are behind, and reaching forth unto those things which are before, I press toward the mark for the prize of the high calling of God in Christ Jesus.

PHILIPPIANS 3:13–14

121.

He brought me up also out of an horrible pit, out of the miry clay, and set my feet upon a rock, and established my goings. And he hath put a new song in my mouth, even praise unto our God: many shall see it, and fear, and shall trust in the LORD.

PSALM 40:2–3

FAITH

God, You are the Alpha and the Omega, the Beginning and the End, the Creator of all things. . .and yet I sometimes lose sight of Your fantastic power. I focus on my weakness and my seemingly insurmountable problems. My faith wavers. Lord, strengthen my faith. My trust in You is the foundation of my belief. Thank You, Jesus, that because of Your sacrifice I am saved by faith. Empower me to walk by faith in the truth and not by sight, which can deceive. By the victory of my faith I can overcome the world! In Jesus name, amen.

122.

Now faith is the substance of things hoped for, the evidence of things not seen. For by it the elders obtained a good report.

HEBREWS 11:1–2

123.

But without faith it is impossible to please him: for he that cometh to God must believe that he is, and that he is a rewarder of them that diligently seek him.

HEBREWS 11:6

124.

Have faith in God. For verily I say unto you,
That whosoever shall say unto this mountain,
Be thou removed, and be thou cast into the sea;
and shall not doubt in his heart, but shall believe
that those things which he saith shall come to
pass; he shall have whatsoever he saith.

MARK 11:22–23

125.

For by grace are ye saved through faith; and
that not of yourselves: it is the gift of God:
Not of works, lest any man should boast.

EPHESIANS 2:8–9

126.

For we walk by faith, not by sight.

2 CORINTHIANS 5:7

127.

And my speech and my preaching was not
with enticing words of man's wisdom, but in
demonstration of the Spirit and of power:
That your faith should not stand in the wisdom
of men, but in the power of God.

1 CORINTHIANS 2:4–5

128.

Knowing that a man is not justified by the works
of the law, but by the faith of Jesus Christ, even
we have believed in Jesus Christ, that we might
be justified by the faith of Christ, and not by the
works of the law: for by the works of the law
shall no flesh be justified.

GALATIANS 2:16

129.

I have fought a good fight, I have finished
my course, I have kept the faith.

2 TIMOTHY 4:7

130.

I am crucified with Christ: nevertheless I live; yet
not I, but Christ liveth in me: and the life which I
now live in the flesh I live by the faith of the Son
of God, who loved me, and gave himself for me.

GALATIANS 2:20

131.

For whatsoever is born of God overcometh
the world: and this is the victory that overcometh
the world, even our faith. Who is he that
overcometh the world, but he that believeth
that Jesus is the Son of God?

1 JOHN 5:4–5

FAITHFULNESS OF GOD

Lord God, a war rages in my soul, and standing firm can be so hard at times. I'm ashamed that my fickle and selfish nature proves victorious more often than I'd like. But You show me undeserved mercy, and no darkness lives in You, God. Psalms says that Your faithfulness stretches to the clouds, Your mercy is everlasting, and Your truth endures forever. Thank You, Jesus, that Your mercy and compassion are new every morning. Great, indeed, is Your faithfulness! In the name of Your precious Son, Jesus, amen.

132.

Thy mercy, O LORD, is in the heavens;
and thy faithfulness reacheth unto the
clouds. Thy righteousness is like the great
mountains; thy judgments are a great deep:
O LORD, thou preservest man and beast.

PSALM 36:5–6

133.

And the LORD passed by before him, and
proclaimed, The LORD, The LORD God, merciful
and gracious, longsuffering, and abundant in
goodness and truth, Keeping mercy for thousands,
forgiving iniquity and transgression and sin.

EXODUS 34:6–7

134.

It is of the Lord's mercies that we are not
consumed, because his compassions fail not.
They are new every morning: great is thy
faithfulness. The Lord is my portion, saith
my soul; therefore will I hope in him.

Lamentations 3:22–24

135.

I will sing of the mercies of the Lord for ever:
with my mouth will I make known thy faithfulness
to all generations. For I have said, Mercy shall
be built up for ever: thy faithfulness shalt thou
establish in the very heavens.

Psalm 89:1–2

136.

Enter into his gates with thanksgiving, and into
his courts with praise: be thankful unto him,
and bless his name. For the Lord is good;
his mercy is everlasting; and his truth
endureth to all generations.

Psalm 100:4–5

137.

The LORD also will be a refuge for the oppressed,
a refuge in times of trouble. And they that know
thy name will put their trust in thee: for thou,
LORD, hast not forsaken them that seek thee.

PSALM 9:9–10

138.

He shall cover thee with his feathers,
and under his wings shalt thou trust:
his truth shall be thy shield and buckler.

PSALM 91:4

139.

Wherefore let them that suffer according to the
will of God commit the keeping of their souls to
him in well doing, as unto a faithful Creator.

1 PETER 4:19

140.

Faithful is he that calleth you,
who also will do it.

1 THESSALONIANS 5:24

———•——————————•———

141.

The LORD hath appeared of old unto me, saying,
Yea, I have loved thee with an everlasting love:
therefore with lovingkindness have I drawn thee.

JEREMIAH 31:3

FEAR

Heavenly Father, I'm afraid. Anxiety threatens my peace. But I know that if I bring You my fears, You will fill me with the assurance of Your promise that You will never leave me. That I am chosen. That I am Yours. That You are my salvation and the strength of my life. All I need to do is open Your Word, and Your peace flows like a river of life into my tortured and barren soul. Thank You, Jesus, that I can lean on You. Thank You for being the light in my darkness. In Jesus' name, amen.

142.

Thou art my servant; I have chosen thee, and not cast thee away. Fear thou not; for I am with thee: be not dismayed; for I am thy God: I will strengthen thee; yea, I will help thee; yea, I will uphold thee with the right hand of my righteousness.

ISAIAH 41:9–10

143.

For God hath not given us the spirit of fear; but of power, and of love, and of a sound mind.

2 TIMOTHY 1:7

144.

For I am persuaded, that neither death, nor
life, nor angels, nor principalities, nor powers,
nor things present, nor things to come,
Nor height, nor depth, nor any other creature,
shall be able to separate us from the love of
God, which is in Christ Jesus our Lord.

ROMANS 8:38–39

145.

The fear of man bringeth a snare: but whoso
putteth his trust in the LORD shall be safe.

PROVERBS 29:25

146.

Be careful for nothing; but in every thing by prayer
and supplication with thanksgiving let your
requests be made known unto God. And the peace
of God, which passeth all understanding, shall
keep your hearts and minds through Christ Jesus.

PHILIPPIANS 4:6–7

147.

Have not I commanded thee? Be strong and
of a good courage; be not afraid, neither be
thou dismayed: for the LORD thy God is
with thee whithersoever thou goest.

JOSHUA 1:9

148.

I sought the LORD, and he heard me,
and delivered me from all my fears.

PSALM 34:4

149.

Fear not: for I have redeemed thee, I have
called thee by thy name; thou art mine.
When thou passest through the waters,
I will be with thee; and through the rivers,
they shall not overflow thee: when thou walkest
through the fire, thou shalt not be burned;
neither shall the flame kindle upon thee.

ISAIAH 43:1–2

150.

The LORD is my light and my salvation;
whom shall I fear? the LORD is the strength
of my life; of whom shall I be afraid?

PSALM 27:1

151.

Fear not them which kill the body, but are not
able to kill the soul: but rather fear him which
is able to destroy both soul and body in hell.

MATTHEW 10:28

FORGIVENESS

Holy God, You have forgiven my sin! You have flung it as far from me as the east is from the west and drowned it in a sea of forgetfulness. Every selfish action, every hurtful word, every wrongdoing, every misstep—gone. Washed clean in the torrent of Your grace and mercy. How could I in turn do any less for those around me? But, Jesus, sometimes I am hurt by others, and it's hard to let go of an offense. Please make me a conqueror. Help me to forgive. In Jesus' cleansing name, amen.

152.

And when ye stand praying, forgive, if ye have ought against any: that your Father also which is in heaven may forgive you your trespasses. But if ye do not forgive, neither will your Father which is in heaven forgive your trespasses.

MARK 11:25–26

153.

If we confess our sins, he is faithful and just to forgive us our sins, and to cleanse us from all unrighteousness.

1 JOHN 1:9

154.

Then came Peter to him, and said, Lord, how oft shall my brother sin against me, and I forgive him? till seven times? Jesus saith unto him, I say not unto thee, Until seven times: but, Until seventy times seven.

MATTHEW 18:21–22

155.

Be ye therefore merciful, as your Father also is merciful. Judge not, and ye shall not be judged: condemn not, and ye shall not be condemned: forgive, and ye shall be forgiven.

LUKE 6:36–37

156.

Forbearing one another, and forgiving one another, if any man have a quarrel against any: even as Christ forgave you, so also do ye.

COLOSSIANS 3:13

157.

He hath not dealt with us after our sins;
nor rewarded us according to our iniquities.
For as the heaven is high above the earth,
so great is his mercy toward them that fear
him. As far as the east is from the west, so far
hath he removed our transgressions from us.

PSALM 103:10–12

158.

I acknowledge my sin unto thee, and mine
iniquity have I not hid. I said, I will confess
my transgressions unto the LORD; and thou
forgavest the iniquity of my sin.

PSALM 32:5

159.

To the praise of the glory of his grace,
wherein he hath made us accepted in the
beloved. In whom we have redemption
through his blood, the forgiveness of sins,
according to the riches of his grace.

EPHESIANS 1:6–7

160.

And they shall teach no more every man his
neighbour, and every man his brother, saying,
Know the LORD: for they shall all know me,
from the least of them unto the greatest of them,
saith the LORD: for I will forgive their iniquity,
and I will remember their sin no more.

JEREMIAH 31:34

161.

Let all bitterness, and wrath, and anger, and
clamour, and evil speaking, be put away from
you, with all malice: And be ye kind one to
another, tenderhearted, forgiving one another,
even as God for Christ's sake hath forgiven you.

EPHESIANS 4:31–32

FREEDOM

Father God, sin can look so enticingly good. It seems to offer such pleasant comfort and satisfaction sometimes. And once indulged, the bars slam shut on my soul and I find myself trapped in a prison of my own desires. But You, Jesus, have set me free. Strengthen my resolve to resist temptation so that I can stand firm in the liberty You have called me to. Your Word has freed me from the strangling bonds of sin and guilt so I can walk unhindered in grace and truth. Thank You, Jesus. Amen.

162.

Stand fast therefore in the liberty wherewith Christ hath made us free, and be not entangled again with the yoke of bondage.

GALATIANS 5:1

163.

For, brethren, ye have been called unto liberty; only use not liberty for an occasion to the flesh, but by love serve one another. For all the law is fulfilled in one word, even in this; Thou shalt love thy neighbour as thyself.

GALATIANS 5:13–14

164.

That with well doing ye may put to silence the ignorance of foolish men: As free, and not using your liberty for a cloke of maliciousness, but as the servants of God. Honour all men. Love the brotherhood. Fear God. Honour the king.

1 Peter 2:15–17

165.

Now the Lord is that Spirit: and where the Spirit of the Lord is, there is liberty. But we all, with open face beholding as in a glass the glory of the Lord, are changed into the same image from glory to glory, even as by the Spirit of the Lord.

2 Corinthians 3:17–18

166.

Then said Jesus to those Jews which believed on him, If ye continue in my word, then are ye my disciples indeed; And ye shall know the truth, and the truth shall make you free.

John 8:31–32

167.

The Spirit of the Lord G<small>OD</small> is upon me;
because the L<small>ORD</small> hath anointed me to
preach good tidings unto the meek; he hath
sent me to bind up the brokenhearted,
to proclaim liberty to the captives, and the
opening of the prison to them that are bound.

I<small>SAIAH</small> 61:1

168.

But now being made free from sin, and
become servants to God, ye have your fruit
unto holiness, and the end everlasting life. For
the wages of sin is death; but the gift of God is
eternal life through Jesus Christ our Lord.

R<small>OMANS</small> 6:22–23

169.

But whoso looketh into the perfect law of
liberty, and continueth therein, he being not
a forgetful hearer, but a doer of the work,
this man shall be blessed in his deed.

J<small>AMES</small> 1:25

170.

For the law of the Spirit of life in Christ Jesus
hath made me free from the law of sin and death.

ROMANS 8:2

———•———————————•———

171.

For ye have not received the spirit of bondage
again to fear; but ye have received the Spirit
of adoption, whereby we cry, Abba, Father.

ROMANS 8:15

GOD'S WORD

God, it seems that the one constant in this life is change. Nothing remains the same, and our circumstances and health and friends are ever in flux. But You have promised us that Your Word is the same forever. Lord, I never have to worry that Your truth has changed. May I steep my mind in the words of scripture so that You light my path and keep me from sin. Your Word is my only truth and a shield around my life that protects me from Satan's lies. In Jesus' name, amen.

172.

The grass withereth, the flower fadeth:
but the word of our God shall stand for ever.

ISAIAH 40:8

———•———•———

173.

For the word of God is quick, and powerful,
and sharper than any twoedged sword, piercing
even to the dividing asunder of soul and spirit,
and of the joints and marrow, and is a discerner
of the thoughts and intents of the heart.

HEBREWS 4:12

174.

All scripture is given by inspiration of God,
and is profitable for doctrine, for reproof,
for correction, for instruction in righteousness:
That the man of God may be perfect,
thoroughly furnished unto all good works.
2 TIMOTHY 3:16–17

175.

In the beginning was the Word, and the
Word was with God, and the Word was God.
The same was in the beginning with God.
JOHN 1:1–2

176.

Sanctify them through thy truth:
thy word is truth.
JOHN 17:17

177.

How sweet are thy words unto my taste!
yea, sweeter than honey to my mouth!
Through thy precepts I get understanding:
therefore I hate every false way. Thy word is a
lamp unto my feet, and a light unto my path.

PSALM 119:103–105

178.

Every word of God is pure: he is a shield
unto them that put their trust in him.
Add thou not unto his words, lest he
reprove thee, and thou be found a liar.

PROVERBS 30:5–6

179.

And the Word was made flesh,
and dwelt among us, (and we beheld his
glory, the glory as of the only begotten
of the Father,) full of grace and truth.

JOHN 1:14

180.

Wherefore lay apart all filthiness and superfluity of naughtiness, and receive with meekness the engrafted word, which is able to save your souls. But be ye doers of the word, and not hearers only, deceiving your own selves.

JAMES 1:21–22

———•————————————•——

181.

So then faith cometh by hearing, and hearing by the word of God.

ROMANS 10:17

GOODNESS

Heavenly Father, let me never doubt Your goodness. Scripture says that every good thing—every single one—originates in You, because You love to bestow good gifts upon Your children. And as Your daughter, I pray that the fruit of Your Spirit's goodness will be evident in my character. You have special tasks lovingly planned for me. Show me the good work You have for me to do today, Father. Rouse joy and strength in my spirit as I work out my faith. In Jesus' name, amen.

182.
But the fruit of the Spirit is love, joy, peace,
longsuffering, gentleness, goodness, faith.
GALATIANS 5:22

183.
And we know that all things work together
for good to them that love God, to them who
are the called according to his purpose.
ROMANS 8:28

184.

Oh how great is thy goodness, which thou
hast laid up for them that fear thee; which
thou hast wrought for them that trust
in thee before the sons of men!

PSALM 31:19

185.

Every good gift and every perfect gift is from
above, and cometh down from the Father of
lights, with whom is no variableness, neither
shadow of turning. Of his own will begat he us
with the word of truth, that we should be a
kind of firstfruits of his creatures.

JAMES 1:17–18

186.

O taste and see that the LORD is good:
blessed is the man that trusteth in him.

PSALM 34:8

187.

And let us not be weary in well doing:
for in due season we shall reap, if we faint
not. As we have therefore opportunity,
let us do good unto all men, especially unto
them who are of the household of faith.

GALATIANS 6:9–10

188.

That they do good, that they be rich in
good works, ready to distribute, willing to
communicate; Laying up in store for themselves a
good foundation against the time to come,
that they may lay hold on eternal life.

1 TIMOTHY 6:18–19

189.

Even so faith, if it hath not works, is dead, being
alone. Yea, a man may say, Thou hast faith, and I
have works: shew me thy faith without thy works,
and I will shew thee my faith by my works.

JAMES 2:17–18

190.

For we are his workmanship, created in Christ Jesus unto good works, which God hath before ordained that we should walk in them.

<small>EPHESIANS 2:10</small>

———•————————————•———

191.

But to do good and to communicate forget not: for with such sacrifices God is well pleased.

<small>HEBREWS 13:16</small>

GRACE

*God, I am humbled by and undeserving of Your grace.
I have sinned against You, Father—many times—even
when I have tried my hardest to please You. But I praise
You, because the very definition of grace is "unmerited
favor." None of us deserves the shockingly extravagant
gift of forgiveness through the sacrifice of Your beloved
Son, Jesus. His blood is a costly and precious gift that
washes away my sins. Thank You, Father, that instead
of the punishment I deserve, You extend grace, mercy,
and forgiveness. In Jesus' name, amen.*

192.
For by grace are ye saved through faith; and
that not of yourselves: it is the gift of God:
Not of works, lest any man should boast.

EPHESIANS 2:8–9

———————•————————————•———

193.
For sin shall not have dominion over you:
for ye are not under the law, but under grace.

ROMANS 6:14

194.

And if by grace, then is it no more of
works: otherwise grace is no more grace.
But if it be of works, then it is no more
grace: otherwise work is no more work.

ROMANS 11:6

195.

But he giveth more grace. Wherefore
he saith, God resisteth the proud,
but giveth grace unto the humble.

JAMES 4:6

196.

But by the grace of God I am what I am:
and his grace which was bestowed upon
me was not in vain; but I laboured more
abundantly than they all: yet not I, but
the grace of God which was with me.

1 CORINTHIANS 15:10

197.

Let us therefore come boldly unto the
throne of grace, that we may obtain mercy,
and find grace to help in time of need.

HEBREWS 4:16

198.

Being justified freely by his grace through
the redemption that is in Christ Jesus: Whom
God hath set forth to be a propitiation through
faith in his blood, to declare his righteousness
for the remission of sins that are past,
through the forbearance of God.

ROMANS 3:24–25

199.

For the grace of God that bringeth salvation
hath appeared to all men, Teaching us that,
denying ungodliness and worldly lusts,
we should live soberly, righteously,
and godly, in this present world.

TITUS 2:11–12

200.

Who hath saved us, and called us with an holy calling, not according to our works, but according to his own purpose and grace, which was given us in Christ Jesus before the world began.

2 TIMOTHY 1:9

201.

The life which I now live in the flesh I live by the faith of the Son of God, who loved me, and gave himself for me. I do not frustrate the grace of God: for if righteousness come by the law, then Christ is dead in vain.

GALATIANS 2:20–21

HEALING

Lord, You are the Great Physician—able to heal not only my body but also to bind up my broken heart and redeem my soul. Because of You, Jesus, I have hope that stretches beyond this fleeting life and into eternity. I ask for Your healing touch, Lord, for nothing lies outside Your power and ability. I will praise You, even if my body in this life remains weak, because I trust that You will strengthen me to endure. And someday when I see You, Jesus, I will have a new and perfect body. In the wondrous name of Jesus, amen.

202.
Fear thou not; for I am with thee: be not dismayed; for I am thy God: I will strengthen thee; yea, I will help thee; yea, I will uphold thee with the right hand of my righteousness.

ISAIAH 41:10

203.
Heal me, O LORD, and I shall be healed; save me, and I shall be saved: for thou art my praise.

JEREMIAH 17:14

204.

Who his own self bare our sins in his own
body on the tree, that we, being dead
to sins, should live unto righteousness:
by whose stripes ye were healed.

1 PETER 2:24

———•————————————•———

205.

He healeth the broken in heart,
and bindeth up their wounds.

PSALM 147:3

———•————————————•———

206.

Is any sick among you? let him call for the
elders of the church; and let them pray over
him, anointing him with oil in the name of
the Lord: And the prayer of faith shall save
the sick, and the Lord shall raise him up.

JAMES 5:14–15

207.

Confess your faults one to another, and pray one for another, that ye may be healed. The effectual fervent prayer of a righteous man availeth much.

JAMES 5:16

208.

The LORD will strengthen him upon the bed of languishing: thou wilt make all his bed in his sickness.

PSALM 41:3

209.

Bless the LORD, O my soul, and forget not all his benefits: Who forgiveth all thine iniquities; who healeth all thy diseases; Who redeemeth thy life from destruction; who crowneth thee with lovingkindness and tender mercies.

PSALM 103:2–4

210.

A merry heart doeth good like a medicine:
but a broken spirit drieth the bones.

PROVERBS 17:22

211.

Have mercy upon me, O LORD; for I am weak:
O LORD, heal me; for my bones are vexed.

PSALM 6:2

HELP

*God, we humans are stubborn and independent
creatures. We find it difficult to admit our inadequacies
to ourselves, let alone ask for help when we need it.
Lord, show me where my stubborn pride has become a
stumbling block. I know that, ultimately, my help comes
from You, but that You also work through the hands
of other believers. Make me humble and gracious in
accepting help and blessings from others, and strengthen
me so that in return I can also assist those in need.
In Jesus' name, amen.*

212.

The LORD shall fight for you,
and ye shall hold your peace.

EXODUS 14:14

213.

Trust in the LORD with all thine heart;
and lean not unto thine own understanding.
In all thy ways acknowledge him,
and he shall direct thy paths.

PROVERBS 3:5–6

214.

I will lift up mine eyes unto the hills,
from whence cometh my help. My help
cometh from the LORD, which made heaven
and earth. He will not suffer thy foot to be
moved: he that keepeth thee will not slumber.

PSALM 121:1–3

215.

Behold, God is mine helper: the Lord
is with them that uphold my soul.

PSALM 54:4

216.

LORD, it is nothing with thee to help, whether
with many, or with them that have no power:
help us, O LORD our God; for we rest on thee, and
in thy name we go against this multitude. O LORD,
thou art our God; let no man prevail against thee.

2 CHRONICLES 14:11

217.

And I will pray the Father, and he shall
give you another Comforter, that he
may abide with you for ever.

JOHN 14:16

218.

The LORD is my strength and my shield;
my heart trusted in him, and I am helped:
therefore my heart greatly rejoiceth;
and with my song will I praise him.

PSALM 28:7

219.

Let us therefore come boldly unto the
throne of grace, that we may obtain mercy,
and find grace to help in time of need.

HEBREWS 4:16

220.
I can do all things through Christ
which strengtheneth me.

PHILIPPIANS 4:13

221.
Yet I will rejoice in the LORD, I will joy in the God
of my salvation. The LORD God is my strength,
and he will make my feet like hinds' feet, and he
will make me to walk upon mine high places.

HABAKKUK 3:18–19

HOPE

*Lord Jesus, without hope this world would be a dark
and depressing pit of despair. You are my hope, Jesus—
my hope for a future, my hope for salvation, my hope
for life. And yet there are people in this world who
don't know Your hope. Through empty eyes they stare
down futures veiled in unrelieved darkness, bleak and
tormented. But You are the Light. Make me a shining
beacon to those oppressed by the enemy. May I live out
my hope in a way that leads others into the light of Your
saving grace. In Jesus' name, amen.*

222.

Rejoicing in hope; patient in tribulation;
continuing instant in prayer.

ROMANS 12:12

223.

For I know the thoughts that I think toward
you, saith the LORD, thoughts of peace,
and not of evil, to give you an expected end.

JEREMIAH 29:11

224.

Now the God of hope fill you with all joy and
peace in believing, that ye may abound in hope,
through the power of the Holy Ghost.

ROMANS 15:13

———•———————————•———

225.

For whatsoever things were written
aforetime were written for our learning,
that we through patience and comfort
of the scriptures might have hope.

ROMANS 15:4

———•———————————•———

226.

And now, Lord, what wait I for?
my hope is in thee.

PSALM 39:7

227.

Blessed be the God and Father of our Lord Jesus Christ, which according to his abundant mercy hath begotten us again unto a lively hope by the resurrection of Jesus Christ from the dead, To an inheritance incorruptible, and undefiled, and that fadeth not away, reserved in heaven for you.

1 PETER 1:3–4

228.

For we are saved by hope: but hope that is seen is not hope: for what a man seeth, why doth he yet hope for? But if we hope for that we see not, then do we with patience wait for it.

ROMANS 8:24–25

229.

But sanctify the Lord God in your hearts: and be ready always to give an answer to every man that asketh you a reason of the hope that is in you with meekness and fear.

1 PETER 3:15

230.

Why art thou cast down, O my soul? and why
art thou disquieted within me? hope in God:
for I shall yet praise him, who is the health
of my countenance, and my God.

PSALM 43:5

231.

Continue in the faith grounded and settled,
and be not moved away from the hope of the
gospel, which ye have heard, and which was
preached to every creature which is under
heaven; whereof I Paul am made a minister.

COLOSSIANS 1:23

HUMILITY

God, You ask me to clothe myself in humility and walk humbly with You. Help me to remember that humility isn't becoming a doormat or failing to stand up for my beliefs, but rather seeing myself and others clearly—as precious sinners. Your Word says that You oppose the proud but show favor to the humble. Lord Jesus, may I always remember the price of grace—Your blood. It's a gift I could never hope to earn. Don't permit me to believe myself better or somehow more deserving than others. In Jesus' name, amen.

232.

Put on therefore, as the elect of God, holy
and beloved, bowels of mercies, kindness,
humbleness of mind, meekness, longsuffering;
Forbearing one another, and forgiving one
another, if any man have a quarrel against any:
even as Christ forgave you, so also do ye.

COLOSSIANS 3:12–13

233.

With all lowliness and meekness, with longsuffering,
forbearing one another in love; endeavouring to
keep the unity of the Spirit in the bond of peace.

EPHESIANS 4:2–3

234.
But he giveth more grace.
Wherefore he saith, God resisteth the
proud, but giveth grace unto the humble.
JAMES 4:6

235.
Humble yourselves in the sight of
the Lord, and he shall lift you up.
JAMES 4:10

236.
If my people, which are called by my name,
shall humble themselves, and pray, and seek
my face, and turn from their wicked ways;
then will I hear from heaven, and will
forgive their sin, and will heal their land.
2 CHRONICLES 7:14

237.

For whosoever exalteth himself shall be abased;
and he that humbleth himself shall be exalted.

LUKE 14:11

238.

He hath shewed thee, O man, what is good;
and what doth the LORD require of thee,
but to do justly, and to love mercy,
and to walk humbly with thy God?

MICAH 6:8

239.

Surely he scorneth the scorners:
but he giveth grace unto the lowly.

PROVERBS 3:34

240.

When pride cometh, then cometh shame:
but with the lowly is wisdom.

PROVERBS 11:2

241.

For I say, through the grace given unto me,
to every man that is among you, not to think
of himself more highly than he ought to think;
but to think soberly, according as God hath
dealt to every man the measure of faith.

ROMANS 12:3

JOY

Lord, may the fruit of joy blossom and ripen in my life. Disease, financial strain, or broken relationships may threaten to pull my eyes from You and shake my security. But I know that Your joy is the bedrock of my strength. You will never be unseated from Your throne. Your power and might are unparalleled. Help me to trust that You love me and are always in control so I will rejoice in You always. My eternal future with You is secure. My joy springs from the knowledge that I am forgiven and loved always. In Jesus' name, amen.

242.

Neither be ye sorry; for the joy
of the LORD is your strength.

NEHEMIAH 8:10

———•——————————•———

243.

But the fruit of the Spirit is love, joy, peace,
longsuffering, gentleness, goodness, faith,
meekness, temperance: against such there is no law.

GALATIANS 5:22–23

244.

Rejoice in the Lord always:
and again I say, Rejoice.

PHILIPPIANS 4:4

245.

Rejoicing in hope; patient in tribulation;
continuing instant in prayer.

ROMANS 12:12

246.

My brethren, count it all joy when ye fall
into divers temptations; Knowing this, that the
trying of your faith worketh patience. But let
patience have her perfect work, that ye may
be perfect and entire, wanting nothing.

JAMES 1:2–4

247.

For ye shall go out with joy, and be led forth
with peace: the mountains and the hills shall
break forth before you into singing, and all the
trees of the field shall clap their hands.

ISAIAH 55:12

248.

We also joy in God through our
Lord Jesus Christ, by whom we
have now received the atonement.

ROMANS 5:11

249.

But let all those that put their trust in thee
rejoice: let them ever shout for joy, because
thou defendest them: let them also that
love thy name be joyful in thee.

PSALM 5:11

250.

Looking unto Jesus the author and finisher of
our faith; who for the joy that was set before him
endured the cross, despising the shame, and is set
down at the right hand of the throne of God.

HEBREWS 12:2

251.

Whom having not seen, ye love; in whom,
though now ye see him not, yet believing,
ye rejoice with joy unspeakable and full of
glory: Receiving the end of your faith,
even the salvation of your souls.

1 PETER 1:8–9

JUSTIFIED

Jesus, it was me. I'm no innocent wrongly charged. I committed crimes of sin against You. Yet through Your blood and startling grace, I am justified. I deserved my punishment, yet You took my whipping on Your own back. My death sentence became Yours—the holy and spotless Passover Lamb. Thank You, Jesus, for paying my penalty and giving me new life in return. No longer a wretched outcast, I'm now an heir with the hope and promise of eternal life. In Jesus' precious name, amen.

252.

According to his mercy he saved us, by the washing of regeneration, and renewing of the Holy Ghost; which he shed on us abundantly through Jesus Christ our Saviour; that being justified by his grace, we should be made heirs according to the hope of eternal life.

TITUS 3:5–7

253.

Therefore being justified by faith, we have peace with God through our Lord Jesus Christ.

ROMANS 5:1

254.

Wherefore the law was our schoolmaster to bring
us unto Christ, that we might be justified by faith.

GALATIANS 3:24

255.

Therefore we conclude that a man is justified
by faith without the deeds of the law.

ROMANS 3:28

256.

Moreover whom he did predestinate,
them he also called: and whom he called,
them he also justified: and whom he
justified, them he also glorified.

ROMANS 8:30

257.

Who was delivered for our offences,
and was raised again for our justification.

ROMANS 4:25

258.

And be found in him, not having mine own
righteousness, which is of the law, but that
which is through the faith of Christ, the
righteousness which is of God by faith.

PHILIPPIANS 3:9

259.

And such were some of you: but ye
are washed, but ye are sanctified,
but ye are justified in the name of the
Lord Jesus, and by the Spirit of our God.

1 CORINTHIANS 6:11

260.

But God commendeth his love toward us, in that, while we were yet sinners, Christ died for us. Much more then, being now justified by his blood, we shall be saved from wrath through him.

ROMANS 5:8–9

261.

We pray you in Christ's stead, be ye reconciled to God. For he hath made him to be sin for us, who knew no sin; that we might be made the righteousness of God in him.

2 CORINTHIANS 5:20–21

KNOWLEDGE

God, I seek to know more about You. The more I learn, the more my awe and wonder of You amplify. Your Word says that the fear of the Lord is the beginning of knowledge. Lord, I offer You my trust and reverence. Teach me more of You, so I can truly worship the amazing and mighty God of the universe. May I never foolishly reject Your wisdom and instruction. Increase my understanding, and guide me over the paths of this life. I choose Your knowledge, which is more precious to my soul than glittering gold. In Jesus' name, amen.

262.
The fear of the LORD is the beginning of knowledge: but fools despise wisdom and instruction. My son, hear the instruction of thy father, and forsake not the law of thy mother: For they shall be an ornament of grace unto thy head, and chains about thy neck.

PROVERBS 1:7–9

263.
For that they hated knowledge, and did not choose the fear of the LORD: They would none of my counsel: they despised all my reproof. Therefore shall they eat of the fruit of their own way, and be filled with their own devices.

PROVERBS 1:29–31

264.

A wise man will hear, and will increase
learning; and a man of understanding
shall attain unto wise counsels.

PROVERBS 1:5

265.

Receive my instruction, and not silver; and
knowledge rather than choice gold. For wisdom
is better than rubies; and all the things that may
be desired are not to be compared to it.

PROVERBS 8:10–11

266.

Teach me good judgment and knowledge:
for I have believed thy commandments.
Before I was afflicted I went astray: but
now have I kept thy word. Thou art good,
and doest good; teach me thy statutes.

PSALM 119:66–68

267.

For I desired mercy, and not sacrifice; and the knowledge of God more than burnt offerings.

HOSEA 6:6

268.

We. . .do not cease to pray for you, and to desire that ye might be filled with the knowledge of his will in all wisdom and spiritual understanding; That ye might walk worthy of the Lord unto all pleasing, being fruitful in every good work, and increasing in the knowledge of God.

COLOSSIANS 1:9–10

269.

Then shalt thou understand the fear of the LORD, and find the knowledge of God. For the LORD giveth wisdom: out of his mouth cometh knowledge and understanding. He layeth up sound wisdom for the righteous: he is a buckler to them that walk uprightly.

PROVERBS 2:5–7

270.

For now we see through a glass, darkly;
but then face to face: now I know in part;
but then shall I know even as also I am known.

1 Corinthians 13:12

———•———————•———

271.

Giving all diligence, add to your faith virtue;
and to virtue knowledge; And to knowledge
temperance; and to temperance patience; and to
patience godliness; And to godliness brotherly
kindness; and to brotherly kindness charity.

2 Peter 1:5–7

LIFESTYLE

Lord Jesus, in this life I can never live up to perfection. I am a broken and sinful person. But I can hope in Your grace and abandon the habits of this world, because You've shown me a better way. Make my actions and attitudes look radically different from those who don't know You, Jesus. Transform my life into a beacon of Your light that pierces the darkness of this world. Examine my ways and help me to discard every thought or word or activity that doesn't please You. In the name of Jesus, amen.

272.

Wherefore gird up the loins of your mind, be sober, and hope to the end for the grace that is to be brought unto you at the revelation of Jesus Christ; As obedient children, not fashioning yourselves according to the former lusts in your ignorance.

1 PETER 1:13–14

———•———————————•———

273.

But as he which hath called you is holy, so be ye holy in all manner of conversation; Because it is written, Be ye holy; for I am holy.

1 PETER 1:15–16

274.

Walk in wisdom toward them that are without, redeeming the time. Let your speech be always with grace, seasoned with salt, that ye may know how ye ought to answer every man.

COLOSSIANS 4:5–6

275.

Now I beseech you, brethren, mark them which cause divisions and offences contrary to the doctrine which ye have learned; and avoid them. For they that are such serve not our Lord Jesus Christ, but their own belly.

ROMANS 16:17–18

276.

Let your conversation be without covetousness; and be content with such things as ye have: for he hath said, I will never leave thee, nor forsake thee.

HEBREWS 13:5

277.

Only let your conversation be as it becometh the gospel of Christ: that whether I come and see you, or else be absent, I may hear of your affairs, that ye stand fast in one spirit, with one mind striving together for the faith of the gospel.

PHILIPPIANS 1:27

278.

Rather let him labour, working with his hands the thing which is good, that he may have to give to him that needeth. Let no corrupt communication proceed out of your mouth, but that which is good to the use of edifying, that it may minister grace unto the hearers.

EPHESIANS 4:28–29

279.

And grieve not the holy Spirit of God, whereby ye are sealed unto the day of redemption. Let all bitterness, and wrath, and anger, and clamour, and evil speaking, be put away from you, with all malice.

EPHESIANS 4:30–31

280.

As strangers and pilgrims, abstain from fleshly lusts, which war against the soul; Having your conversation honest among the Gentiles: that, whereas they speak against you as evildoers, they may by your good works, which they shall behold, glorify God in the day of visitation.

1 Peter 2:11–12

281.

Whatsoever things are true, whatsoever things are honest, whatsoever things are just, whatsoever things are pure, whatsoever things are lovely, whatsoever things are of good report; if there be any virtue, and if there be any praise, think on these things.

Philippians 4:8

LOVE

Heavenly Father, You are love. You flood our world
with Your incredible love for Your children. . .for me,
Lord. Thank You for loving me in spite of my flaws.
Even when I cringe at my actions and think, Don't
look, Jesus, You're not shocked or surprised. You love
me anyway. You still died to save me. And Your greatest
commandment is that I, in return, offer You and those
around me that same awe-inspiring, borderless love. Fill
me with the power of Your Holy Spirit, God, so that I
too can love without limits. In Jesus' name, amen.

282.
He that loveth not knoweth
not God; for God is love.
1 John 4:8

283.
Master, which is the great commandment
in the law? Jesus said unto him, Thou shalt
love the Lord thy God with all thy heart,
and with all thy soul, and with all thy mind.
Matthew 22:36–37

284.

Charity suffereth long, and is kind; charity envieth not; charity vaunteth not itself, is not puffed up, Doth not behave itself unseemly, seeketh not her own, is not easily provoked, thinketh no evil; Rejoiceth not in iniquity, but rejoiceth in the truth; Beareth all things, believeth all things, hopeth all things, endureth all things. Charity never faileth.

1 CORINTHIANS 13:4–8

285.

This is my commandment, That ye love one another, as I have loved you. Greater love hath no man than this, that a man lay down his life for his friends. Ye are my friends, if ye do whatsoever I command you.

JOHN 15:12–14

286.

For God so loved the world, that he gave his only begotten Son, that whosoever believeth in him should not perish, but have everlasting life. For God sent not his Son into the world to condemn the world; but that the world through him might be saved.

JOHN 3:16–17

287.

He that hath my commandments, and keepeth them, he it is that loveth me: and he that loveth me shall be loved of my Father, and I will love him, and will manifest myself to him.

JOHN 14:21

288.

We love him, because he first loved us. If a man say, I love God, and hateth his brother, he is a liar: for he that loveth not his brother whom he hath seen, how can he love God whom he hath not seen?

1 JOHN 4:19–20

289.

A new commandment I give unto you, That ye love one another; as I have loved you, that ye also love one another. By this shall all men know that ye are my disciples, if ye have love one to another.

JOHN 13:34–35

290.

Put on therefore, as the elect of God, holy
and beloved, bowels of mercies, kindness,
humbleness of mind, meekness, longsuffering;
Forbearing one another, and forgiving one
another, if any man have a quarrel against any:
even as Christ forgave you, so also do ye.
And above all these things put on charity,
which is the bond of perfectness.

COLOSSIANS 3:12–14

———•————————•———

291.

My little children, let us not love in word,
neither in tongue; but in deed and in truth.

1 JOHN 3:18

MERCY

Lord God, Your limitless mercy is a healing balm to my soul. It soothes my aching fears and kindles hope within me that I haven't strayed too far—that I haven't crossed a point of no return, where Your mercy and grace don't reach. Lord, Your Word says that You desire mercy over sacrifice, life over death. Lead me in the way of mercy, Father, so that I extend Your mercy to others. It's so easy to desire retribution when I am wronged, but I must remember how my sins have drowned in the tides of Your mercy. Amen.

292.

Be ye therefore merciful,
as your Father also is merciful.

LUKE 6:36

293.

Blessed are the merciful:
for they shall obtain mercy.

MATTHEW 5:7

294.

But go ye and learn what that meaneth, I will have mercy, and not sacrifice: for I am not come to call the righteous, but sinners to repentance.

MATTHEW 9:13

295.

Let us therefore come boldly unto the throne of grace, that we may obtain mercy, and find grace to help in time of need.

HEBREWS 4:16

296.

So speak ye, and so do, as they that shall be judged by the law of liberty. For he shall have judgment without mercy, that hath shewed no mercy; and mercy rejoiceth against judgment.

JAMES 2:12–13

297.

Blessed be the God and Father of our Lord Jesus Christ, which according to his abundant mercy hath begotten us again unto a lively hope by the resurrection of Jesus Christ from the dead, To an inheritance incorruptible, and undefiled, and that fadeth not away, reserved in heaven for you.

1 Peter 1:3–4

298.

Bless the Lord, O my soul, and forget not all his benefits: Who forgiveth all thine iniquities; who healeth all thy diseases; Who redeemeth thy life from destruction; who crowneth thee with lovingkindness and tender mercies.

Psalm 103:2–4

299.

If we confess our sins, he is faithful and just to forgive us our sins, and to cleanse us from all unrighteousness.

1 John 1:9

300.

This I recall to my mind, therefore have I hope. It is of the Lord's mercies that we are not consumed, because his compassions fail not. They are new every morning: great is thy faithfulness.

LAMENTATIONS 3:21–23

301.

But after that the kindness and love of God our Saviour toward man appeared, not by works of righteousness which we have done, but according to his mercy he saved us, by the washing of regeneration, and renewing of the Holy Ghost.

TITUS 3:4–5

MIGHTY GOD

*God, at times I'm guilty of forgetting just who You are—
the First and the Last, the almighty God, controller of the
vast universe, all-powerful, all-seeing, all-knowing. . . .
My fragile human mind sometimes puts You in a box
defined by my limited understanding of Your power, but
I know You are so much greater than what I can com-
prehend. I know that nothing escapes Your ability. Lord,
when I worry and fear my circumstances, help me to
rest in Your strong arms and trust that You've got this. . .
that Your will be done. In Jesus' name, amen.*

302.

I am Alpha and Omega, the beginning and the
ending, saith the Lord, which is, and which was,
and which is to come, the Almighty.

REVELATION 1:8

303.

For unto us a child is born, unto us a son is
given: and the government shall be upon
his shoulder: and his name shall be called
Wonderful, Counsellor, The mighty God,
The everlasting Father, The Prince of Peace.

ISAIAH 9:6

304.

In the beginning was the Word, and the
Word was with God, and the Word was God.
The same was in the beginning with God.
All things were made by him; and without
him was not any thing made that was made.

JOHN 1:1–3

305.

In the beginning God created the heaven
and the earth. And the earth was without
form, and void; and darkness was upon the
face of the deep. And the Spirit of God moved
upon the face of the waters. And God said,
Let there be light: and there was light.

GENESIS 1:1–3

306.

But to us there is but one God, the Father,
of whom are all things, and we in him;
and one Lord Jesus Christ, by whom
are all things, and we by him.

1 CORINTHIANS 8:6

307.

For the LORD your God is God of gods, and Lord
of lords, a great God, a mighty, and a terrible,
which regardeth not persons, nor taketh reward.

DEUTERONOMY 10:17

308.

And God said unto Moses, I AM THAT I AM:
and he said, Thus shalt thou say unto the
children of Israel, I AM hath sent me unto you.

EXODUS 3:14

309.

For by him were all things created, that
are in heaven, and that are in earth, visible
and invisible, whether they be thrones,
or dominions, or principalities, or powers:
all things were created by him, and for him:
And he is before all things, and by
him all things consist.

COLOSSIANS 1:16–17

310.

Thus saith the LORD the King of Israel, and his redeemer the LORD of hosts; I am the first, and I am the last; and beside me there is no God.

ISAIAH 44:6

311.

Thus saith the LORD, thy redeemer, and he that formed thee from the womb, I am the LORD that maketh all things; that stretcheth forth the heavens alone; that spreadeth abroad the earth by myself.

ISAIAH 44:24

PATIENCE

Jesus, patience is not a strength I have mastered. Why, when You have shown me limitless patience, am I so impatient with those around me? I want things to happen now, and I don't want to be bothered with others' problems because they might interfere with my own agenda. Lord, forgive me. I haven't shown Your Spirit's patience toward the world. I have been self-centered. Increase my love and compassion toward others so that patience will be stirred in my heart. Help me to patiently work out Your plans. In the precious and powerful name of Jesus, amen.

312.

Rejoicing in hope; patient in tribulation;
continuing instant in prayer.

ROMANS 12:12

313.

He shall bring forth thy righteousness as the light,
and thy judgment as the noonday. Rest in the LORD,
and wait patiently for him: fret not thyself because
of him who prospereth in his way, because of the
man who bringeth wicked devices to pass.

PSALM 37:6–7

314.

Charity suffereth long, and is kind.

1 CORINTHIANS 13:4

315.

But they that wait upon the LORD shall renew
their strength; they shall mount up with
wings as eagles; they shall run, and not be
weary; and they shall walk, and not faint.

ISAIAH 40:31

316.

The Lord is not slack concerning his promise,
as some men count slackness; but is longsuffering
to us-ward, not willing that any should perish,
but that all should come to repentance.

2 PETER 3:9

317.

Be patient therefore, brethren, unto the coming
of the Lord. Behold, the husbandman waiteth
for the precious fruit of the earth, and hath long
patience for it, until he receive the early and latter
rain. Be ye also patient; stablish your hearts:
for the coming of the Lord draweth nigh.

JAMES 5:7–8

318.

But the fruit of the Spirit is love, joy, peace,
longsuffering, gentleness, goodness, faith.

GALATIANS 5:22

319.

Put on therefore, as the elect of God,
holy and beloved, bowels of mercies,
kindness, humbleness of mind, meekness,
longsuffering; Forbearing one another,
and forgiving one another.

COLOSSIANS 3:12–13

320.

Now we exhort you, brethren, warn them
that are unruly, comfort the feebleminded,
support the weak, be patient toward all men.

1 Thessalonians 5:14

———•————————————•———

321.

And we desire that every one of you do shew
the same diligence to the full assurance of hope
unto the end: That ye be not slothful, but
followers of them who through faith and
patience inherit the promises.

Hebrews 6:11–12

PEACE

Lord, it seems we have but one certainty in this world: it will rain. Gale-force winds will howl, and life will get dicey. Our minds will flood with uncertainties and fears, but in the midst of those turbulent waters, You are the Prince of Peace who leads us beside quiet streams. The disciples screamed in terror when it seemed the storm would overtake them, but You, Jesus, peacefully slept. And when they woke You, You said, "Be still." Jesus, fill my heart and mind with the stillness of Your peace, no matter what torment rages around me. Amen.

322.

These things I have spoken unto you, that in me ye might have peace. In the world ye shall have tribulation: but be of good cheer; I have overcome the world.

JOHN 16:33

323.

Thou wilt keep him in perfect peace, whose mind is stayed on thee: because he trusteth in thee. Trust ye in the LORD for ever: for in the LORD JEHOVAH is everlasting strength.

ISAIAH 26:3–4

324.

And let the peace of God rule in your
hearts, to the which also ye are called
in one body; and be ye thankful.

COLOSSIANS 3:15

325.

For they that are after the flesh do mind
the things of the flesh; but they that are after
the Spirit the things of the Spirit. For to
be carnally minded is death; but to be
spiritually minded is life and peace.

ROMANS 8:5–6

326.

Great peace have they which love thy law:
and nothing shall offend them.

PSALM 119:165

327.

Be careful for nothing; but in every thing by prayer and supplication with thanksgiving let your requests be made known unto God. And the peace of God, which passeth all understanding, shall keep your hearts and minds through Christ Jesus.

PHILIPPIANS 4:6–7

328.

Therefore being justified by faith, we have peace with God through our Lord Jesus Christ: By whom also we have access by faith into this grace wherein we stand, and rejoice in hope of the glory of God.

ROMANS 5:1–2

329.

And the work of righteousness shall be peace; and the effect of righteousness quietness and assurance for ever.

ISAIAH 32:17

330.

Behold the fowls of the air: for they sow not,
neither do they reap, nor gather into barns;
yet your heavenly Father feedeth them.
Are ye not much better than they?

MATTHEW 6:26

331.

Blessed are the peacemakers: for they
shall be called the children of God.

MATTHEW 5:9

PERSEVERANCE

Lord, distractions abound in this world. If Satan cannot turn us from following You, he is at least content to distract us from Your cause. Keep my focus on You, Jesus. This world entices with temporary comforts, but You offer eternal rewards and true life that will never end. Plant me firmly in the foundation of Your Word so the enemy's lies will not sway me. Give me steadfast devotion to You, Jesus, so I run my race well and win the crown. I long to hear You say, "Well done, my good and faithful servant." In Jesus' name, amen.

332.

Blessed is the man that endureth temptation:
for when he is tried, he shall receive the crown
of life, which the Lord hath promised
to them that love him.

JAMES 1:12

333.

And let us not be weary in well doing: for
in due season we shall reap, if we faint not.

GALATIANS 6:9

334.

We glory in tribulations also: knowing that
tribulation worketh patience; and patience,
experience; and experience, hope: And hope
maketh not ashamed; because the love of God
is shed abroad in our hearts by the Holy
Ghost which is given unto us.

Romans 5:3–5

335.

My brethren, count it all joy when ye fall into
divers temptations; knowing this, that the trying
of your faith worketh patience. But let patience
have her perfect work, that ye may be perfect
and entire, wanting nothing.

James 1:2–4

336.

Being confident of this very thing, that he
which hath begun a good work in you will
perform it until the day of Jesus Christ.

Philippians 1:6

337.

Seek the LORD and his strength, seek his face continually. Remember his marvellous works that he hath done, his wonders, and the judgments of his mouth.

1 CHRONICLES 16:11–12

338.

For ye have need of patience, that, after ye have done the will of God, ye might receive the promise.

HEBREWS 10:36

339.

Seeing we also are compassed about with so great a cloud of witnesses, let us lay aside every weight, and the sin which doth so easily beset us, and let us run with patience the race that is set before us, Looking unto Jesus the author and finisher of our faith.

HEBREWS 12:1–2

340.

Behold, I come quickly: hold that fast which
thou hast, that no man take thy crown. Him that
overcometh will I make a pillar in the temple of
my God, and he shall go no more out.

REVELATION 3:11–12

———•————————•———

341.

And ye shall be hated of all men for
my name's sake: but he that endureth
to the end shall be saved.

MATTHEW 10:22

PRAYER

Heavenly Father, Your Word says to pray always about everything. But sometimes I forget. I rush around in my busy life and try to take care of everything myself. Forgive me, Father, for neglecting to have a conversation with You. You created me and this world and set Your plans in motion; and here I am trying to bend my circumstances to my will without even consulting the master designer. Lord, I want to talk to You more. I need Your direction and wisdom to navigate this world. In the name of Jesus, amen.

342.

Pray without ceasing.

1 THESSALONIANS 5:17

343.

The Spirit also helpeth our infirmities: for we know not what we should pray for as we ought: but the Spirit itself maketh intercession for us with groanings which cannot be uttered.

ROMANS 8:26

344.

But thou, when thou prayest, enter into thy
closet, and when thou hast shut thy door, pray
to thy Father which is in secret; and thy Father
which seeth in secret shall reward thee openly.

MATTHEW 6:6

345.

Call unto me, and I will answer thee,
and show thee great and mighty things,
which thou knowest not.

JEREMIAH 33:3

346.

Watch and pray, that ye enter not into temptation:
the spirit indeed is willing, but the flesh is weak.

MATTHEW 26:41

347.

Confess your faults one to another, and pray one for another, that ye may be healed. The effectual fervent prayer of a righteous man availeth much.

JAMES 5:16

348.

Praying always with all prayer and supplication in the Spirit, and watching thereunto with all perseverance and supplication for all saints.

EPHESIANS 6:18

349.

The righteous cry, and the LORD heareth, and delivereth them out of all their troubles.

PSALM 34:17

350.

Continue in prayer, and watch
in the same with thanksgiving.

COLOSSIANS 4:2

———•————————•———

351.

Our Father which art in heaven, Hallowed be
thy name. Thy kingdom come, Thy will be done
in earth, as it is in heaven. Give us this day our
daily bread. And forgive us our debts, as we
forgive our debtors. And lead us not into
temptation, but deliver us from evil.

MATTHEW 6:9–13

PRIDE

God, my pride is deceptive and sly. My thoughts wander, and suddenly I become aware of some aspect of my life to feel prideful about. My mind bends naturally to comparison and loves to find the areas where I shine. But Your kingdom is different, Jesus. With You, the least is the greatest and the first is last. You reward the humble and oppose the proud. Jesus, I am unworthy of Your love, and my sin is great, but You saved me anyway. Keep me vigilant in curbing my pride so I may walk in humility and kindness. Amen.

352.

When pride cometh, then cometh shame:
but with the lowly is wisdom.

PROVERBS 11:2

353.

Pride goeth before destruction, and an
haughty spirit before a fall. Better it is to
be of an humble spirit with the lowly,
than to divide the spoil with the proud.

PROVERBS 16:18–19

354.

But he giveth more grace. Wherefore
he saith, God resisteth the proud,
but giveth grace unto the humble.

JAMES 4:6

355.

For if a man think himself to be something,
when he is nothing, he deceiveth himself.

GALATIANS 6:3

356.

For all that is in the world, the lust of the flesh,
and the lust of the eyes, and the pride of life,
is not of the Father, but is of the world.

1 JOHN 2:16

357.

Let nothing be done through strife or vainglory; but in lowliness of mind let each esteem other better than themselves.

PHILIPPIANS 2:3

358.

Be of the same mind one toward another. Mind not high things, but condescend to men of low estate. Be not wise in your own conceits.

ROMANS 12:16

359.

Humble yourselves in the sight of the Lord, and he shall lift you up.

JAMES 4:10

360.

Blessed are the poor in spirit:
for theirs is the kingdom of heaven.

MATTHEW 5:3

361.

For whosoever exalteth himself shall be abased;
and he that humbleth himself shall be exalted.

LUKE 14:11

PROTECTION

Lord, You are the Mighty God, the commander of heavenly armies. You are my rock in a world filled with quicksand, my shelter in the storms that I know will come my way. Your peace guards my heart and mind like a midnight watcher on a castle wall. Your protection comforts my soul. Keep me safe from evil and physical harm as I navigate this often treacherous world. Thank You, Jesus, for the promise that You will never leave me nor forsake me. I am not alone. In the powerful name of Jesus, amen.

362.
He that dwelleth in the secret place of the most High shall abide under the shadow of the Almighty. I will say of the Lord, He is my refuge and my fortress: my God; in him will I trust.

PSALM 91:1–2

363.
The angel of the Lord encampeth round about them that fear him, and delivereth them.

PSALM 34:7

364.

God is our refuge and strength, a very present help in trouble. Therefore will not we fear, though the earth be removed, and though the mountains be carried into the midst of the sea; Though the waters thereof roar and be troubled, though the mountains shake with the swelling thereof.

PSALM 46:1–3

365.

But the Lord is faithful, who shall stablish you, and keep you from evil.

2 THESSALONIANS 3:3

366.

Yea, though I walk through the valley of the shadow of death, I will fear no evil: for thou art with me; thy rod and thy staff they comfort me.

PSALM 23:4

367.

The name of the LORD is a strong tower:
the righteous runneth into it, and is safe.

PROVERBS 18:10

368.

The LORD is my rock, and my fortress, and my
deliverer; The God of my rock; in him will I trust:
he is my shield, and the horn of my salvation,
my high tower, and my refuge, my saviour;
thou savest me from violence.

2 SAMUEL 22:2–3

369.

There hath no temptation taken you but such as
is common to man: but God is faithful, who will
not suffer you to be tempted above that ye are
able; but will with the temptation also make a
way to escape, that ye may be able to bear it.

1 CORINTHIANS 10:13

370.

I have called thee by thy name; thou art mine.
When thou passest through the waters, I will
be with thee; and through the rivers, they shall
not overflow thee: when thou walkest through
the fire, thou shalt not be burned; neither
shall the flame kindle upon thee.

ISAIAH 43:1–2

371.

But thou, O LORD, art a shield for me;
my glory, and the lifter up of mine head.

PSALM 3:3

RECONCILIATION

God, it's Your great desire that I live in peace with You and with other people, especially my fellow believers in Christ. I know my sins create a rift between You and me. Compared to Your brilliant and perfect glory, my heart is tattered and stained by my wrongdoings. But through Your mercy, You wash away my grime so I become as white as new-fallen snow. Thank You, Jesus, that because of You I am reconciled with my God. Lord, soften my heart and bring reconciliation to my relationships as well. In Jesus' name, amen.

372.

Come now, and let us reason together, saith the Lord: though your sins be as scarlet, they shall be as white as snow; though they be red like crimson, they shall be as wool.

ISAIAH 1:18

373.

When we were enemies, we were reconciled to God by the death of his Son, much more, being reconciled, we shall be saved by his life. And not only so, but we also joy in God through our Lord Jesus Christ, by whom we have now received the atonement.

ROMANS 5:10–11

374.

Having made peace through the blood of his cross, by him to reconcile all things unto himself; by him, I say, whether they be things in earth, or things in heaven. And you, that were sometime alienated and enemies in your mind by wicked works, yet now hath he reconciled.

COLOSSIANS 1:20–21

375.

Follow peace with all men, and holiness, without which no man shall see the Lord.

HEBREWS 12:14

376.

And above all things have fervent charity among yourselves: for charity shall cover the multitude of sins.

1 PETER 4:8

377.

Forbearing one another, and forgiving one
another, if any man have a quarrel against any:
even as Christ forgave you, so also do ye.

COLOSSIANS 3:13

378.

For all have sinned, and come short of the glory
of God; Being justified freely by his grace through
the redemption that is in Christ Jesus.

ROMANS 3:23–24

379.

For God so loved the world, that he
gave his only begotten Son, that whosoever
believeth in him should not perish, but
have everlasting life. For God sent not his
Son into the world to condemn the world; but
that the world through him might be saved.

JOHN 3:16–17

380.

To wit, that God was in Christ, reconciling the world unto himself, not imputing their trespasses unto them; and hath committed unto us the word of reconciliation.

2 CORINTHIANS 5:19

381.

But now in Christ Jesus ye who sometimes were far off are made nigh by the blood of Christ. For he is our peace, who hath made both one, and hath broken down the middle wall of partition between us.

EPHESIANS 2:13–14

REPENTANCE

Jesus, when You began Your ministry here on earth, You said, "Repent, for the kingdom of heaven has arrived." You call me to change my life and turn away from my sins, because You brought God's kingdom to earth. Lord, my sins can be so enticing. Strengthen me to leave them behind and embrace Your kingdom living today. I no longer want the empty things I used to chase. Their shine has dulled, and their appeal has turned to dust in comparison to the sparkling glory of living in Your kingdom. In Jesus' name, amen.

382.

From that time Jesus began to preach, and to say, Repent: for the kingdom of heaven is at hand.

MATTHEW 4:17

———•————————•———

383.

Those things, which God before had shewed by the mouth of all his prophets, that Christ should suffer, he hath so fulfilled. Repent ye therefore, and be converted, that your sins may be blotted out, when the times of refreshing shall come from the presence of the Lord.

ACTS 3:18–19

384.

The Lord is not slack concerning his promise,
as some men count slackness; but is longsuffering
to us-ward, not willing that any should perish,
but that all should come to repentance.

2 PETER 3:9

385.

Then Peter said unto them, Repent, and be
baptized every one of you in the name of Jesus
Christ for the remission of sins, and ye shall
receive the gift of the Holy Ghost.

ACTS 2:38

386.

And the times of this ignorance God winked at;
but now commandeth all men every where to
repent: Because he hath appointed a day, in the
which he will judge the world in righteousness
by that man whom he hath ordained.

ACTS 17:30–31

387.

Thinkest thou this, O man, that judgest them which do such things, and doest the same, that thou shalt escape the judgment of God? Or despisest thou the riches of his goodness and forbearance and longsuffering; not knowing that the goodness of God leadeth thee to repentance?

ROMANS 2:3–4

388.

When they heard these things, they held their peace, and glorified God, saying, Then hath God also to the Gentiles granted repentance unto life.

ACTS 11:18

389.

Bring forth therefore fruits meet for repentance: And think not to say within yourselves, We have Abraham to our father: for I say unto you, that God is able of these stones to raise up children unto Abraham.

MATTHEW 3:8–9

390.

For godly sorrow worketh repentance
to salvation not to be repented of: but
the sorrow of the world worketh death.

2 CORINTHIANS 7:10

391.

He that covereth his sins shall not prosper:
but whoso confesseth and forsaketh
them shall have mercy.

PROVERBS 28:13

REST

Lord, You offer priceless gifts to me. This world can be heavy and wearying. But You want me to have rest. Rest and peace for my soul—an internal oasis in the midst of this gale-force life. Jesus, teach me to abide in You, to remain and be present with You always—regardless of my circumstances. In my joy or in my pain, in peace or in chaos, my soul is at rest in You. When my anxiety heightens, remind me to turn to You in prayer, Jesus. . . to offload my burdens and be led by still waters. Amen.

392.
Come unto me, all ye that labour and are heavy laden, and I will give you rest. Take my yoke upon you, and learn of me; for I am meek and lowly in heart: and ye shall find rest unto your souls.
MATTHEW 11:28–29

393.
And he said, My presence shall go with thee, and I will give thee rest.
EXODUS 33:14

394.

It is vain for you to rise up early,
to sit up late, to eat the bread of sorrows:
for so he giveth his beloved sleep.

PSALM 127:2

395.

Rest in the LORD, and wait patiently for
him: fret not thyself because of him who
prospereth in his way, because of the man
who bringeth wicked devices to pass.

PSALM 37:7

396.

For thus saith the Lord GOD, the Holy
One of Israel; In returning and rest
shall ye be saved; in quietness and in
confidence shall be your strength.

ISAIAH 30:15

397.

For I have satiated the weary soul, and I
have replenished every sorrowful soul.

JEREMIAH 31:25

398.

But they that wait upon the LORD shall
renew their strength; they shall mount up
with wings as eagles; they shall run, and not
be weary; and they shall walk, and not faint.

ISAIAH 40:31

399.

Thus saith the LORD, Stand ye in the ways,
and see, and ask for the old paths, where
is the good way, and walk therein, and
ye shall find rest for your souls.

JEREMIAH 6:16

400.

Thou wilt keep him in perfect peace, whose mind
is stayed on thee: because he trusteth in thee.

Isaiah 26:3

401.

Remember the sabbath day, to keep it holy.
Six days shalt thou labour, and do all thy work:
But the seventh day is the sabbath of the Lord
thy God: in it thou shalt not do any work.

Exodus 20:8–10

REWARDS

God, we all love rewards, achievements, and winning.
But my efforts are wasted if I'm striving toward the wrong
goals—if I win my prize only to discover that its profits
are empty and meaningless. But Your rewards won't
disappoint me, God, because they offer eternal returns.
Help me to keep my eyes fixed on Your kingdom, Jesus.
This world offers much, but it cannot give me eternity,
nor does it deal in the currency of peace and hope.
May I run my race well and win the ultimate prize—
eternal life with You. In the name of Jesus, amen.

402.

Every man's work shall be made manifest: for the
day shall declare it, because it shall be revealed
by fire; and the fire shall try every man's work of
what sort it is. If any man's work abide which he
hath built thereupon, he shall receive a reward.

1 CORINTHIANS 3:13–14

403.

Blessed is the man that endureth temptation:
for when he is tried, he shall receive the crown
of life, which the Lord hath promised
to them that love him.

JAMES 1:12

404.

And whatsoever ye do, do it heartily, as to the Lord, and not unto men; Knowing that of the Lord ye shall receive the reward of the inheritance: for ye serve the Lord Christ.

COLOSSIANS 3:23–24

405.

Judge nothing before the time, until the Lord come, who both will bring to light the hidden things of darkness, and will make manifest the counsels of the hearts: and then shall every man have praise of God.

1 CORINTHIANS 4:5

406.

And when the chief Shepherd shall appear, ye shall receive a crown of glory that fadeth not away.

1 PETER 5:4

407.

His lord said unto him, Well done, good and
faithful servant; thou hast been faithful over a few
things, I will make thee ruler over many things:
enter thou into the joy of thy lord.

MATTHEW 25:23

408.

Henceforth there is laid up for me a crown of
righteousness, which the Lord, the righteous
judge, shall give me at that day: and not to me
only, but unto all them also that love his appearing.

2 TIMOTHY 4:8

409.

For we must all appear before the judgment
seat of Christ; that every one may receive the
things done in his body, according to that he
hath done, whether it be good or bad.

2 CORINTHIANS 5:10

410.

I go to prepare a place for you. And if I go
and prepare a place for you, I will come
again, and receive you unto myself; that
where I am, there ye may be also.

JOHN 14:2–3

411.

But now being made free from sin, and
become servants to God, ye have your fruit
unto holiness, and the end everlasting life. For
the wages of sin is death; but the gift of God is
eternal life through Jesus Christ our Lord.

ROMANS 6:22–23

SALVATION

God, as I walk through my years on this earth I more fully grasp the importance of Your precious forgiveness. My mess-ups and problems seem to accumulate like garbage in a dump. I'm helpless to erase them or take away the sting of so many mistakes. But I don't have to. Thank You, Jesus, that You forgive my sins. That You cast them into a sea of forgetfulness and clothe me in pristine white robes. No other name can save me, Jesus. Only Yours—the Christ, the Son of the living God, the Lamb. In the saving name of Jesus I pray, amen.

412.

Not by works of righteousness which we have done, but according to his mercy he saved us, by the washing of regeneration, and renewing of the Holy Ghost; Which he shed on us abundantly through Jesus Christ our Saviour.

TITUS 3:5–6

413.

For by grace are ye saved through faith; and that not of yourselves: it is the gift of God: Not of works, lest any man should boast.

EPHESIANS 2:8–9

414.

That if thou shalt confess with thy mouth
the Lord Jesus, and shalt believe in thine
heart that God hath raised him from
the dead, thou shalt be saved.

ROMANS 10:9

—•————————•—

415.

Jesus saith unto him, I am the way,
the truth, and the life: no man cometh
unto the Father, but by me.

JOHN 14:6

—•————————•—

416.

This is the stone which was set at nought of you
builders, which is become the head of the corner.
Neither is there salvation in any other: for there
is none other name under heaven given among
men, whereby we must be saved.

ACTS 4:11–12

417.

But the salvation of the righteous is of the LORD:
he is their strength in the time of trouble.

PSALM 37:39

418.

For God so loved the world, that he gave his
only begotten Son, that whosoever believeth
in him should not perish, but have everlasting
life. For God sent not his Son into the world
to condemn the world; but that the world
through him might be saved.

JOHN 3:16–17

419.

I do not frustrate the grace of God:
for if righteousness come by the law,
then Christ is dead in vain.

GALATIANS 2:21

420.

But God, who is rich in mercy, for his great love wherewith he loved us, Even when we were dead in sins, hath quickened us together with Christ, (by grace ye are saved;) And hath raised us up together, and made us sit together in heavenly places in Christ Jesus.

EPHESIANS 2:4–6

———•————————•———

421.

Verily, verily, I say unto you, He that heareth my word, and believeth on him that sent me, hath everlasting life, and shall not come into condemnation; but is passed from death unto life.

JOHN 5:24

SELF-CONTROL

Lord God, in a do-what-feels-good world, self-control is often frowned upon and even discouraged. But I know, God, that out of Your great love for us, You've given Your commands for our own benefit and happiness. To live a joyful life is to follow Your laws; and trying to go my own way and make up my own rules will lead only to dysfunction and pain. You tell us to grow up in our faith and be self-controlled—to tame our urges and our bodies like an athlete in training. I delight in Your laws, Lord Jesus. Amen.

422.

He that hath no rule over his own spirit is like a city that is broken down, and without walls.

PROVERBS 25:28

423.

Giving all diligence, add to your faith virtue; and to virtue knowledge; And to knowledge temperance; and to temperance patience; and to patience godliness; And to godliness brotherly kindness; and to brotherly kindness charity.

2 PETER 1:5–7

424.

Know ye not that they which run in a race
run all, but one receiveth the prize? So run,
that ye may obtain. And every man that striveth
for the mastery is temperate in all things.
Now they do it to obtain a corruptible crown;
but we an incorruptible.

1 CORINTHIANS 9:24–25

425.

For God hath not given us the spirit of fear;
but of power, and of love, and of a sound mind.

2 TIMOTHY 1:7

426.

But I keep under my body, and bring it into
subjection: lest that by any means, when I have
preached to others, I myself should be a castaway.

1 CORINTHIANS 9:27

427.

He that is slow to anger is better than
the mighty; and he that ruleth his
spirit than he that taketh a city.

PROVERBS 16:32

428.

But the end of all things is at hand: be ye
therefore sober, and watch unto prayer.

1 PETER 4:7

429.

For the grace of God that bringeth salvation
hath appeared to all men, Teaching us that,
denying ungodliness and worldly lusts,
we should live soberly, righteously,
and godly, in this present world.

TITUS 2:11–12

430.

I beseech you therefore, brethren, by the
mercies of God, that ye present your bodies
a living sacrifice, holy, acceptable unto God,
which is your reasonable service.

ROMANS 12:1

———•———————————————•———

431.

And be not conformed to this world: but be
ye transformed by the renewing of your mind,
that ye may prove what is that good, and
acceptable, and perfect, will of God.

ROMANS 12:2

SHAME

Jesus, I've done things I'm not proud of. My sins condemn me like the religious leaders who threatened to stone the adulterous woman. But You didn't condemn her. Instead, You stepped into the circle of their accusations with her, and You forgave her. Just as You have forgiven me. Thank You, Jesus, that You've wiped away my shame and replaced it with the joy of knowing Your grace and mercy. I am clean! In the precious name of Jesus, amen.

432.

For your shame ye shall have double; and for confusion they shall rejoice in their portion: therefore in their land they shall possess the double: everlasting joy shall be unto them.

ISAIAH 61:7

433.

If we confess our sins, he is faithful and just to forgive us our sins, and to cleanse us from all unrighteousness.

1 JOHN 1:9

434.

They looked unto him, and were lightened:
and their faces were not ashamed.

PSALM 34:5

435.

For the scripture saith, Whosoever
believeth on him shall not be ashamed.

ROMANS 10:11

436.

There is therefore now no condemnation to
them which are in Christ Jesus, who walk
not after the flesh, but after the Spirit.

ROMANS 8:1

437.

Fear not; for thou shalt not be ashamed:
neither be thou confounded; for thou shalt
not be put to shame: for thou shalt forget the
shame of thy youth, and shalt not remember
the reproach of thy widowhood any more.
For thy Maker is thine husband.

ISAIAH 54:4–5

438.

Come now, and let us reason together, saith
the LORD: though your sins be as scarlet, they
shall be as white as snow; though they be red
like crimson, they shall be as wool.

ISAIAH 1:18

439.

What fruit had ye then in those things whereof
ye are now ashamed? for the end of those things
is death. But now being made free from sin, and
become servants to God, ye have your fruit unto
holiness, and the end everlasting life.

ROMANS 6:21–22

440.

And such were some of you: but ye are
washed, but ye are sanctified, but ye are
justified in the name of the Lord Jesus,
and by the Spirit of our God.

1 CORINTHIANS 6:11

STRENGTH

Lord God Almighty, You bolster me with new strength when I am weak. When I stumble and my faith trembles with the strain of a single forward shuffle, You are there. You are the all-powerful God of the universe, and You have promised that I am not on this faith journey alone. Lend me Your strength each day as I work out my faith, Lord. Give me the energy I need to do the work You have planned for me and the desire and will to choose Your way. In Jesus' name, amen.

441.

The LORD is good, a strong hold in the day of trouble; and he knoweth them that trust in him.

NAHUM 1:7

442.

Fear thou not; for I am with thee: be not dismayed; for I am thy God: I will strengthen thee; yea, I will help thee; yea, I will uphold thee with the right hand of my righteousness.

ISAIAH 41:10

443.

I can do all things through
Christ which strengtheneth me.

PHILIPPIANS 4:13

444.

For the LORD your God is he that goeth with you,
to fight for you against your enemies, to save you.

DEUTERONOMY 20:4

445.

The LORD is my strength and song, and he
is become my salvation: he is my God,
and I will prepare him an habitation;
my father's God, and I will exalt him.

EXODUS 15:2

446.

My grace is sufficient for thee: for my strength
is made perfect in weakness. Most gladly
therefore will I rather glory in my infirmities,
that the power of Christ may rest upon me.

2 CORINTHIANS 12:9

447.

Therefore I take pleasure in infirmities,
in reproaches, in necessities, in persecutions,
in distresses for Christ's sake: for when
I am weak, then am I strong.

2 CORINTHIANS 12:10

448.

Seek the LORD and his strength,
seek his face continually.

1 CHRONICLES 16:11

449.

He giveth power to the faint; and to them
that have no might he increaseth strength.

ISAIAH 40:29

———•————————————•———

450.

The Lord stood with me,
and strengthened me.

2 TIMOTHY 4:17

TEMPTATION

Jesus, deliver me from this temptation. Your Word says that we will never be tempted beyond what we can bear, that You will always provide a way of escape. Lord, show me my exit strategy. The enemy knows my weakness and uses it against me. Give me Your words to fight back. You answered Satan's temptations with scripture, Jesus. Fill my mind with God's laws so I can stand strong against Satan's lies. Help me to meditate day and night on the Word of God so it will illuminate my path. In the name of Jesus, amen.

451.

There hath no temptation taken you but such as is common to man: but God is faithful, who will not suffer you to be tempted above that ye are able; but will with the temptation also make a way to escape, that ye may be able to bear it.

1 Corinthians 10:13

452.

Now for a season, if need be, ye are in heaviness through manifold temptations: That the trial of your faith, being much more precious than of gold that perisheth, though it be tried with fire, might be found unto praise and honour and glory at the appearing of Jesus Christ.

1 Peter 1:6–7

453.

For though we walk in the flesh, we do not war after the flesh: (For the weapons of our warfare are not carnal, but mighty through God to the pulling down of strong holds.)

2 CORINTHIANS 10:3–4

454.

Casting down imaginations, and every high thing that exalteth itself against the knowledge of God, and bringing into captivity every thought to the obedience of Christ.

2 CORINTHIANS 10:5

455.

Watch and pray, that ye enter not into temptation: the spirit indeed is willing, but the flesh is weak.

MATTHEW 26:41

456.

Let no man say when he is tempted, I am tempted of God: for God cannot be tempted with evil, neither tempteth he any man: But every man is tempted, when he is drawn away of his own lust, and enticed.

JAMES 1:13–14

457.

Then when lust hath conceived, it bringeth forth sin: and sin, when it is finished, bringeth forth death.

JAMES 1:15

458.

Submit yourselves therefore to God. Resist the devil, and he will flee from you.

JAMES 4:7

459.

For in that he himself hath suffered
being tempted, he is able to
succour them that are tempted.

HEBREWS 2:18

460.

Neither yield ye your members as instruments
of unrighteousness unto sin: but yield
yourselves unto God, as those that are alive
from the dead, and your members as
instruments of righteousness unto God.

ROMANS 6:13

TRUST

Lord, trusting You can be so difficult when I've been conditioned to believe that I need to blaze my own trail and take care of everything myself. But Your Word says if I trust in You, You will direct my paths and that Your plans for my future are good. I trust in Your promises. I trust in Your good nature—You are a good Father. Give me steadfast trust even when I don't understand why certain things happen. You are still in control, Lord God of the universe. And Your plans will be accomplished. In Jesus' name, amen.

461.

Trust in the LORD with all thine heart;
and lean not unto thine own understanding.
In all thy ways acknowledge him,
and he shall direct thy paths.

PROVERBS 3:5–6

462.

For I know the thoughts that I think toward
you, saith the LORD, thoughts of peace, and
not of evil, to give you an expected end.

JEREMIAH 29:11

463.

My son, forget not my law; but let thine
heart keep my commandments: For length
of days, and long life, and peace, shall they
add to thee. Let not mercy and truth forsake
thee: bind them about thy neck; write
them upon the table of thine heart.

PROVERBS 3:1–3

464.

But I have trusted in thy mercy; my heart shall
rejoice in thy salvation. I will sing unto the LORD,
because he hath dealt bountifully with me.

PSALM 13:5–6

465.

Blessed is that man that maketh the
LORD his trust, and respecteth not the
proud, nor such as turn aside to lies.

PSALM 40:4

466.

Thou wilt keep him in perfect peace, whose mind is stayed on thee: because he trusteth in thee. Trust ye in the LORD for ever: for in the LORD JEHOVAH is everlasting strength.

ISAIAH 26:3–4

467.

And they that know thy name will put their trust in thee: for thou, LORD, hast not forsaken them that seek thee.

PSALM 9:10

468.

He shall not be afraid of evil tidings: his heart is fixed, trusting in the LORD.

PSALM 112:7

469.
It is better to trust in the LORD
than to put confidence in man.
PSALM 118:8

————•————————————•————

470.
He staggered not at the promise of God through
unbelief; but was strong in faith, giving glory to
God; And being fully persuaded that, what he
had promised, he was able also to perform. And
therefore it was imputed to him for righteousness.
ROMANS 4:20–22

TRUTH

Jesus, the world says that truth is whatever I want it to be—that absolute truth is a myth, and we can select our truth as we would food from a buffet line. Pick what looks the most scrumptious or what you're craving. But You said, "I am the way, the truth, and the life. No one comes to the Father except through me" (John 14:6). I know that You are the one-way street that leads to eternal life and joy. The enemy's lies hold no sway over me when I compare them to Your words. Protect me from counterfeit "truth." Amen.

471.

Jesus saith unto him, I am the
way, the truth, and the life: no man
cometh unto the Father, but by me.

JOHN 14:6

472.

And ye shall know the truth,
and the truth shall make you free.

JOHN 8:32

473.
They are not of the world, even as I am
not of the world. Sanctify them through
thy truth: thy word is truth.

JOHN 17:16–17

474.
Study to shew thyself approved unto God,
a workman that needeth not to be ashamed,
rightly dividing the word of truth.

2 TIMOTHY 2:15

475.
Wherefore take unto you the whole armour of
God, that ye may be able to withstand in the
evil day, and having done all, to stand. Stand
therefore, having your loins girt about with truth.

EPHESIANS 6:13–14

476.

My little children, let us not love in word,
neither in tongue; but in deed and in truth.
And hereby we know that we are of the truth,
and shall assure our hearts before him.

1 JOHN 3:18–19

477.

Thy word is true from the beginning: and every
one of thy righteous judgments endureth for ever.

PSALM 119:160

478.

And the Word was made flesh, and dwelt
among us, (and we beheld his glory, the
glory as of the only begotten of the Father,)
full of grace and truth.

JOHN 1:14

479.

Every good gift and every perfect gift is from above, and cometh down from the Father of lights, with whom is no variableness, neither shadow of turning. Of his own will begat he us with the word of truth, that we should be a kind of firstfruits of his creatures.

JAMES 1:17–18

480.

But speaking the truth in love, may grow up into him in all things, which is the head, even Christ.

EPHESIANS 4:15

UNDERSTANDING

God, You sent Your Holy Spirit to be our comforter and teacher. Sometimes I read things in Your Word that I don't understand. Instruct me in Your ways, Father. Give me understanding and insight into the meaning of scripture. I want to know You more and live by Your laws. Show me more of You, so our relationship can grow roots that spread deep and strong. I long for greater understanding, because the more I learn about You the greater my love is for You. In the name of Your precious Son, Jesus, amen.

481.

A fool hath no delight in understanding,
but that his heart may discover itself.

PROVERBS 18:2

482.

The entrance of thy words giveth light;
it giveth understanding unto the simple.
I opened my mouth, and panted: for I
longed for thy commandments.

PSALM 119:130–131

483.

Yea, if thou criest after knowledge, and liftest up thy voice for understanding; If thou seekest her as silver, and searchest for her as for hid treasures; Then shalt thou understand the fear of the LORD, and find the knowledge of God.

PROVERBS 2:3–5

484.

Happy is the man that findeth wisdom, and the man that getteth understanding. For the merchandise of it is better than the merchandise of silver, and the gain thereof than fine gold.

PROVERBS 3:13–14

485.

But the Comforter, which is the Holy Ghost, whom the Father will send in my name, he shall teach you all things.

JOHN 14:26

486.

Consider what I say; and the Lord give
thee understanding in all things.

2 TIMOTHY 2:7

487.

We have received, not the spirit of the world, but
the spirit which is of God; that we might know
the things that are freely given to us of God.

1 CORINTHIANS 2:12

488.

Which things also we speak, not in the
words which man's wisdom teacheth,
but which the Holy Ghost teacheth;
comparing spiritual things with spiritual.

1 CORINTHIANS 2:13

489.

Having the understanding darkened,
being alienated from the life of God
through the ignorance that is in them,
because of the blindness of their heart.

EPHESIANS 4:18

490.

Thus saith the LORD, Let not the wise man glory
in his wisdom, neither let the mighty man glory
in his might, let not the rich man glory in his
riches: But let him that glorieth glory in this,
that he understandeth and knoweth me.

JEREMIAH 9:23–24

WISDOM

Heavenly Father, we often get our priorities in a jumble here on earth. We spend our days accumulating things or experiences or power. And we attempt to find lasting meaning and worth in the idols we've pursued. But You said that wisdom is more precious than rubies. Lord, grant me Your wisdom—wisdom to see what holds its value in Your kingdom and wisdom to become more like Jesus. I've engaged in the world's sprint to the top, but Your kingdom is a race to the bottom, where the least are crowned. In Jesus' name, amen.

491.

For wisdom is better than rubies;
and all the things that may be desired
are not to be compared to it.

PROVERBS 8:11

492.

If any of you lack wisdom, let him ask of
God, that giveth to all men liberally, and
upbraideth not; and it shall be given him.

JAMES 1:5

493.

And be not conformed to this world: but be ye transformed by the renewing of your mind, that ye may prove what is that good, and acceptable, and perfect, will of God.

ROMANS 12:2

494.

For the LORD giveth wisdom: out of his mouth cometh knowledge and understanding. He layeth up sound wisdom for the righteous: he is a buckler to them that walk uprightly.

PROVERBS 2:6–7

495.

And unto man he said, Behold, the fear of the LORD, that is wisdom; and to depart from evil is understanding.

JOB 28:28

496.

But the wisdom that is from above is first
pure, then peaceable, gentle, and easy to be
intreated, full of mercy and good fruits,
without partiality, and without hypocrisy.

JAMES 3:17

———•————————————•———

497.

See then that ye walk circumspectly, not as fools,
but as wise, Redeeming the time, because the
days are evil. Wherefore be ye not unwise, but
understanding what the will of the Lord is.

EPHESIANS 5:15–17

———•————————————•———

498.

The fear of the LORD is the beginning
of knowledge: but fools despise
wisdom and instruction.

PROVERBS 1:7

499.
Let the word of Christ dwell in you richly in all
wisdom; teaching and admonishing one another
in psalms and hymns and spiritual songs, singing
with grace in your hearts to the Lord.

Colossians 3:16

———•————————————•———

500.
Through wisdom is an house builded;
and by understanding it is established:
And by knowledge shall the chambers be
filled with all precious and pleasant riches.

Proverbs 24:3–4

NEW *BIBLE PROMISE BOOK*®
EDITIONS COMING SOON

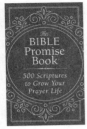